The hunger for depth and meaning

John Main OSB (1926-1982)
Portrait by Brenda Bury

The hunger for depth and meaning

Learning to meditate with John Main

Edited by Peter Ng

Medio Media

Published 2007 in Singapore
by Medio Media
www.mediomedia.org
mmi@wccm.org

© The World Community for Christian Meditation 2007

Cover Photograph by Thorsten Ulonska, www.ulonska.net
Book Design by Subsonic Media, Germany, www.subsonicmedia.de
Portrait of John Main by Brenda Bury

ISBN 978-1-933182-63-6

All rights reserved

No part of this book may be reproduced, stored in a retrieval system, or transmitted, in any form or by any means, electronic, mechanical, photocopying, recording or otherwise without the written permission of Medio Media

Medio Media is the publishing arm of
The World Community for Christian Meditation

The World Community for Christian Meditation
International Centre
St Mark's, Myddelton Square
London EC1R 1XX, UK
www.wccm.org

Printed in Singapore by
Stamford Press Pte Ltd

In memory of

my wife Patricia

and

in gratitude to

my friend Laurence Freeman OSB

who led me to John Main

Contents

About this Book	10
John Main and Christian Prayer	12
Foreword	15
Preface	18

1 THE ESSENCE — 25

1.1 Fullness of Being	26
1.2 Leaving the Ego Behind	29
1.3 Discovering Our Potential	32
1.4 Ultimate Meaning	34
1.5 Expansion of Being	36
1.6 Re-linked to Our Centre	38

2 THE PRACTICE — 41

2.1 How to Meditate	42
2.2 The Basic Doctrine	43
2.3 Times of Meditation	45
2.4 Distractions	48
2.5 Preparations to Meditate	51

3 THE THEOLOGY — 53

3.1 The Theology of Prayer	54
3.2 Only One Prayer	56
3.3 Beyond All Concepts of God	58
3.4 To Lose Ourselves in Christ	61
3.5 God's Mysterious Presence within Us	63
3.6 The Birth of Christ in Our Hearts	65
3.7 Transformation of Human Consciousness	68
3.8 Death and Resurrection	71

4 THE MANTRA 74

- 4.1 The Grand Poverty of the Mantra — 75
- 4.2 Choosing Your Mantra — 77
- 4.3 Stages of Saying the Mantra — 79
- 4.4 Saying and Sounding the Mantra — 81
- 4.5 Listening to the Mantra — 84
- 4.6 Say Your Mantra until You Cannot Say It — 86
- 4.7 Breathing and the Mantra — 88

5 THE TRADITION 90

- 5.1 What the Tradition Tells Us — 91
- 5.2 The Tradition of the Mantra — 94
- 5.3 Purity of Heart — 97
- 5.4 John Cassian — 100
- 5.5 The Mantra in Christian Prayer — 102

6 THE JOURNEY 104

- 6.1 Set Your Mind on the Kingdom — 105
- 6.2 Self-Transcendence — 107
- 6.3 To Persevere — 109
- 6.4 Meditation as an Art — 110
- 6.5 Without Expectations — 112
- 6.6 Psychical Phenomena — 114
- 6.7 Progress in the Stillness — 116
- 6.8 Not My Way but The Way — 118
- 6.9 The Ultimate Aim of Meditation — 120

7 THE FRUITS — 122

- 7.1 Living in the Present Moment — 123
- 7.2 Learning to Be — 125
- 7.3 Abandonment of Desire — 127
- 7.4 Detachment — 129
- 7.5 Liberty of Spirit — 131
- 7.6 Freedom — 132
- 7.7 Growing in Love — 134
- 7.8 Rooted in God — 137
- 7.9 Personal Harmony — 139
- 7.10 Mature Relationships — 141
- 7.11 Christian Community — 143
- 7.12 Other-Centredness — 146
- 7.13 Meaning, Significance, and Purpose — 149
- 7.14 Stability — 151
- 7.15 Fullness of Life — 153
- 7.16 Values System Based on God — 155

8 THE WAY — 158

- 8.1 The Way of Silence — 159
- 8.2 The Way of Stillness — 162
- 8.3 The Way of Simplicity — 165
- 8.4 The Way of Discipline — 168
- 8.5 The Way of Commitment — 170
- 8.6 The Way of Leaving Self Behind — 173
- 8.7 The Way of Faith — 175
- 8.8 The Way of Trust — 179
- 8.9 The Way of Love — 182
- 8.10 The Way of Wisdom — 185
- 8.11 The Way of Enlightenment — 188
- 8.12 The Way of Peace — 191
- 8.13 The Way of Attention — 194

Works by and about John Main 197
    Books 197
    CDs / Cassette Tapes 199

About The World Community for Christian Meditation 200
The World Community For Christian Meditation Centres/
Contacts Worldwide 202

About this Book

This book is composed of sixty-nine extracts from John Main's spoken teachings, arranged thematically in eight sections. The extracts offer a clear and comprehensive overview of the teaching on prayer by one of the spiritual masters of the twentieth century. The recordings from which these extracts have been taken are published by Medio Media, the publishing and communication arm of The World Community for Christian Meditation. We have worked hard to improve the technical quality of the recordings and many of them have now been digitalized.

The extracts in this book correspond with John Main's original spoken word on a set of ten CDs under the same title as this book: *The Hunger for Depth and Meaning*. His very contemporary Christian contemplative teaching addresses people in all walks of life. It touches their spiritual anguish as they struggle to make sense of their lives.

Many of the early monastic teachers, like Evagrius Ponticus in the fourth century, avoided long abstract teachings and preferred the format of short, pithy sayings or 'chapters' which could be chewed over and even memorized by their disciples. And John Main taught meditation in the ancient Christian tradition.

This book can therefore be used as inspiration and encouragement for the twice-daily practice of meditation. Meditators may read through it systematically to steadily absorb a broad but deep understanding of the tradition. Or they may read it selectively, taking one or more extracts at a time, to prepare for or to conclude their times of meditation. The repetition of several themes is intentional, because a spiritual learning process does not aim at constant novelty of ideas but rather at an ever-deeper penetration and understanding of truth.

The book can also be used profitably at group meetings in conjunction with the CDs. For easy reference, the talks on the CDs are arranged under the same titles and in the same order as in the book. For additional convenience, the duration of each talk is also indicated. Typically, a weekly Christian Meditation group begins with a talk by John Main as preparation for a period of silent meditation. After meditation the group often reflects together on the teaching and how it illumines their own continuing spiritual journey.

John Main and Christian Prayer

One of the most influential spiritual teachers of prayer of our time was the Irish Benedictine monk John Main. He was born in England in 1926 and died in Canada fifty-six years later. For Fr Bede Griffiths, writing soon after John Main's death, he was the "most important spiritual guide in the church today".

As a young Catholic working as a diplomat in the Far East, John Main was introduced to meditation by a gentle Hindu monk Swami Satyananda. Never swaying from his own Christian faith, John Main immediately recognized the value of this practice that deepened and enriched the other forms of Christian prayer. It was not until years later that he fully realized how deeply this silent prayer of the heart was rooted in his own Christian tradition. He saw with fresh eyes the teachings of Jesus on prayer. And he read anew John Cassian's vivid descriptions of the early Christian monks, the Desert Fathers and Mothers, who practised and taught by their own humble example the simple discipline of *monologistos*, the 'prayer of one word'. He saw how powerfully this discipline deals with the distractions that inevitably fill the mind, most obviously at the time of prayer, but at other times as well.

In the mantra he saw the way to that stillness (*hesychia* as the Eastern Christians called it) or 'pure prayer', that is 'worship in spirit and truth'. He saw how the discipline of the mantra purifies the heart of contradictory desires and unifies us. The place of unity is the heart where we find the deepest and most natural orientation towards God as our personal source and goal. He understood too how the mantra brings us to poverty of spirit, or the non-possessiveness that Jesus set as the first beatitude and the primary condition of human happiness.

John Main soon learned through his own practice of meditation that the morning and evening discipline of meditation balances the whole day, every day of one's life, in an ever-deepening peace and joy. And, more and more, he saw the connection between this experience of inner peace and joy with the gospel and Christian faith. Prayer for him now appeared as much more than speaking to or thinking about God. It is being with God.

John Main also saw the quality of our relationships as the true measure of progress in meditation. He knew that progress was in the end an accomplishment of grace. But again, we must do our part. We must respond to the call of grace not with a mere technique, but with a discipline of faith. For John Main, as for the centuries-old Christian tradition he spoke from, a freely chosen discipline is the path to freedom not bondage. Spiritual discipline is a valuable necessity in the work of being free from the tyranny of egotism, compulsiveness, delusion and self-centredness.

He was therefore always very clear that meditation is a way of faith, and very practical about how and when it must be practised. The minimal commitment to individual meditation twice a day and group meditation once a week is only the external aspect of the discipline John Main taught. He knew that most people begin the discipline of meditation half-heartedly, or with a tremendous zeal that inevitably, like any enthusiasm, weakens. We begin, then stop and then begin again, often many times. It takes time, maybe years, for some people to incorporate the basic discipline of meditation in their daily lives.

That is just why a meditation group is so valuable. Not many people are good at self-discipline entirely on their own. It takes time and continual encouragement to build a good habit. Through the support and example of others, we strengthen our insight that meditation is simple, but not easy; life-giving, not life-denying; and most of all, a way of love. For all these reasons John Main encouraged people who wanted to learn to meditate and to keep on meditating to cultivate the gifts of community that grow among those who share the journey of prayer. Hence the formation and persistence of more than a thousand groups of three or six or twenty, meeting weekly in churches, homes, offices, hospitals, hospices, prisons, colleges, schools and shopping malls.

Foreword

It is twenty-five years since Fr John died. Twenty-five years since his spirit began to expand through his teaching and through the community, very small as it then was, that had already come to be born through the silence of meditation. He had only been teaching meditation publicly for seven years. He had met strong responses, both positive and negative, but for those seven years he had steered a clear, straight course ahead in the full confidence of his faith and his deep sense of mission. He had found his life's purpose and in those few years he lived the full fruit of his whole life-experience in a total self-giving to this work, in a self-abandonment of great courage and love.

This morning after meditation I listened to two of his talks and I am amazed still, as I write, at the power and clarity of what he taught. How extraordinarily simple and luminous. How painfully and joyfully direct. How unchanged by the passage of a generation is the freshness and urgency of his message.

I know of no other teaching in this form that carries the spirit of the gospel, the living Word, so directly and purely straight into the heart. His voice varies over the years the tapes were made. In the early ones you hear the physical vigour and passion of his full teaching authority. In the talks recorded in his last months of life one hears his voice grow weaker. But there is a different kind of strength. As his health failed his inner light burned more intensely and even the silences between the phrases of his talks are filled with a power that takes his words deeper into the mind and heart of the listener.

Almost every talk has a scripture passage as its inspiration and launch-pad. It takes off into rich variations of his essential themes illustrated by and rooted in his own experience. Every talk is new each time one hears it. At its root is the passionate conviction of the Gospel's invitation to fullness of life, to full liberty of spirit. Meditation is the way to realize this through experiential not merely speculative knowledge. He believed in the need for clear thought and the right use of the intellect but he knew it was not the essence. Even in this life, he said, we can experience something of the torrent of love that is the internal dynamism of the Trinity. "The generous immensity we call God", he called it.

What did I find so inspiring and moving this morning as I listened to Fr John's voice? I think it was the gentleness and love in his call not to compromise, not to downplay our potential but to respond as absolutely as possible to the divine love that penetrates and pervades our being and all our experience. What is also so staggering is the simplicity of his conviction that the way is the way of the mantra. He points to this not as an escape from the challenge to be one but as a way of becoming one. It is a way of concentration not dispersion.

> *If only we could learn the simplicity of saying the word in childlike faith we would lose ourselves in God and find our way into relationship with all, into love.*

After twenty-five years as a community we might be at the stage of losing energy and getting into a rut. If we are not, it is simply due to the purity and simplicity of the message I heard in the words and the silences of Fr John's tapes this morning. We have to live more deeply the detachment he taught and lived. If we are to move into what seems to me the coming third phase of our life as a community we must be prepared for change, new forms. It is all a manifestation of the same mysterious presence of the Lord whose birth we have just celebrated and who is born more deeply in us each time we meditate.

The message Fr John and we are given to share with the world is more urgently needed than ever. A new generation must receive it and each of us is called – as a priority and as part of our own journey – to do the best we can to make sure they hear it. The joyful power of Fr John's teaching is that he makes it so clear what this vision is and what it means.

Laurence Freeman OSB
Director, The World Community for Christian Meditation

Preface

I began working on this book three years ago in June 2003. Soon after, my wife Patricia and I were shocked to discover that she was gravely ill with late-stage stomach cancer. This was to be the greatest challenge for us as life-partners. The initial prognosis was that she might not survive beyond a few months. But she courageously faced the illness. The nineteen months before she died began in panic, but unfolded as a journey into peace. It was paradoxically the happiest time of our lives as husband and wife.

John Main spoke of meditation as our first death, the death of the ego, and saw meditation as an essential preparation for our second and final death. As meditators, Patricia and I had experienced the fruits of meditation in the art of living. But it was our journey from panic to peace that revealed the power of meditation in the art of dying.

When asked by Fr Laurence Freeman how meditation was helping her to cope with the illness, she responded, "I didn't think it worked until now when it's working. When you meditate, you don't see the effects and you keep thinking, 'I am still the same old bad self,' and ' My meditation is still full of distractions' or ' I'm not getting visions or anything dramatic'. But, in times of crisis like this, when I can't understand why I'm getting so much peace, then I know that all those years of practice is really bearing fruit when I need it ." *

Patricia and I had been led to meditation eighteen years earlier. It was a time in our lives when we were searching for a meaningful spiritual path. At the level of material needs, we were then

---

* *From Panic to Peace*, a DVD published by Medio Media, presents Patricia in conversation with Fr Laurence Freeman and Peter Ng as she reflects on the meaning of life, death, suffering, faith, relationships and community in the light of her experience with cancer and the practice of meditation.

quite contented. Our standard of living well exceeded what we had expected in our youth. I was doing well in my career and enjoying tremendously the job of investing money. Family life was joyful. Our two children, Terence and Deborah, were entering their teenage years. Patricia had stopped working in a bank five years earlier to spend more time with them. She was feeling quite fulfilled in the experience of motherhood. Yet there was for both of us a restlessness amidst the material contentment. Somehow we felt there must be more to life than that. We were searching for a spiritual path that could bring more meaning into our lives. Perhaps this feeling was what Fr Laurence, in his introduction to *Light Within* called an "unidentifiable anguish of the spirit straining beyond the superficiality and meaninglessness of modern life-styles" and opening the mind to the "need to journey to the heart".

Our spiritual search led us to observe that meditation was an essential practice in the Buddhist and Hindu traditions. As Christians, we wondered whether there was a similar way of prayer but rooted in the Christian tradition. On a visit to the church bookshop, soon after our interest in meditation was aroused, Patricia's eyes fell on *Light Within* the moment she stepped inside the door. We were both very excited about the discovery, especially Patricia, as she immediately began to meditate in the way recommended in the book. I postponed the journey, preferring to wait until we had a chance to meet some of the people involved in the teaching. Soon we had the opportunity to visit the London Meditation Centre. Our meeting with Sr Madeleine, and the first experience of meditating with a group there, strongly kindled the flame of interest. I returned to Singapore resolved to begin the journey.

It was, as Fr John said, simple but not easy. Even before taking on the daunting challenge of being mentally still, just to be still physically proved to be more difficult than I had thought. I began by sitting on a chair, but then thought it would be more reverent and perhaps more comfortable to sit on the floor. It made no difference to the agitated state of body and mind. Twenty minutes, let alone thirty, seemed impossible. To avoid giving up altogether I shortened the period of meditation to ten minutes. Distractions were a great source of discouragement. The silence of meditation was fertile ground for dreaming and planning. Most of us live such an outward life that, when we first begin to learn to meditate, those times of prayer start off as extensions of our outward concerns. I wondered when I would begin that inner journey. For a whole year, I struggled with countless false starts. The difficulty of entering the stillness of meditation, coupled with the continuing demands of a busy executive and family life, meant that I meditated when I could and felt like doing it, rather than when I should. It was always easy to find excuses for the frequent lapses. What really encouraged me to hang on was Patricia's perseverance in treading the path which constantly reminded me of my own calling.

The critical juncture of my journey was in February 1988 when Fr Laurence visited Singapore on his way to Australia. It was our first meeting with him. I still remember our waving his book at the airport so that he could identify us. We arranged with our parish priest, Fr Alfred Chan, for Fr Laurence to give a talk to the parishioners at Holy Family Church. About four hundred people attended. We were astounded by the huge turn-out, and we could feel that the period of meditation after the talk brought a new dimension of worship in our church. Before he left Singapore, Fr Laurence suggested that we should get a weekly group going. With the enthusiasm of the moment I agreed that it was a reasonable follow-up to the good response at his talk. The next day, as I mulled over the proposition, I recoiled on realising that I was poorly prepared for the task of starting a group. I could not honestly explain to a group that the teaching was that they should meditate every day, twice a day, and for at least twenty minutes each time, when I myself fell well short of this discipline. In that dilemma I realized that the time had come for me to make a commitment. I would have to re-order the priorities in my life. For three weeks I somehow found the time for morning and evening meditation and the fortitude to endure the mental distractions and physical discomfort. I found that the discipline was possible. We now have 27 groups in 18 parishes. I have found that the work of starting and leading groups has been the greatest source of encouragement and sustenance for my own journey. I have discovered, too, that the most important requirement to passing on the teaching effectively is my own fidelity to the discipline.

How has meditation changed my life? Fr Laurence has said it is very difficult to suggest how the saying of the mantra can so powerfully transform one's life and be felt in every relationship, in every project one undertakes, and in the work one does. Nonetheless, he suggests that "simply saying the mantra commits us to living out the consequences of saying the mantra. We can't meditate every day and continue to pursue a policy of deception, of self-interest, of revenge. However gradually, we must also begin to commit ourselves in daily life to truthfulness, to love, to God." Fr Laurence went on to explain that the core of Fr John's teaching is that we must first learn to be and then we will know what to do. What we do is only changed deeply and permanently by what we are. These are truths that I have learned from the journey of meditation. The way to silence, stillness and simplicity is the way *of* silence, stillness and simplicity. The way to commitment and discipline is the way *of* commitment and discipline. The way to faith and love is the way *of* faith and love. To reach the destination one must be on the way. Meditation is the way.

I now have a glimpse of what Father John meant when he said that meditation would add a dimension of incredible richness and be the great integrating power in one's life, giving depth and perspective to everything we are and everything we do. Gently but steadily, there has been a reorientation in the direction of life.

Priorities become clear. Trivialities are either dropped or fade away. I feel an energizing balance beginning to harmonize work, family life, physical well-being and the spiritual life.

The process of living itself has been enriched. For example, it is incredible how the daily practice of selfless attention in the saying of the mantra can permeate the activities of the day. I have found that when I can bring this attentive awareness to the things I do such as walking, reading, golfing, it puts me in deeper touch with the present moment of life and with the world of creation. One begins to appreciate the pure gift of life.

In the last forty years of youth and adulthood I have had many pursuits whether professional, social or spiritual, in which sooner or later I lost interest. I still wonder why I have been able to maintain the commitment to meditation. The richness and the authority of the teaching of Fr John and Fr Laurence have been a constant source of inspiration and nourishment. But, above all, I suspect that it is the self-authenticating experience of meditation that keeps me on the way. Only by meditation can one experience and understand it as a journey of faith and love. Only by meditating can one sense the inner transformation as well as the manifestation of the fruits of meditation in one's daily life.

In regard to the teaching; I have been particularly inspired by several statements of Fr John which express his insight that the way of meditation is rooted in the Gospel message. He explains that to meditate is to be in the indwelling presence of the Holy Spirit. The aim of prayer is to leave our prayers behind so that we may join the prayer of Christ whose Spirit is constantly praying within us. Meditation is our answer to the call of Jesus to leave self behind and follow him in discipleship. Fr John saw meditation as our response to the love and the generosity of God: a generosity revealed in the Incarnation and the life of Jesus, a selflessness that accepted death on the cross. Meditation is our way to that same generosity. Our meditation enables us to offer ourselves entirely, in our wholeness, to God. It is perhaps the greatest thing that we can do as conscious human beings – to offer our consciousness to God. I did not have the opportunity of meeting Fr John, but I have been moved so much by the power and authority in his voice on the *Communitas* tapes.

My struggle in embarking, and persevering, on the journey of meditation was greatly helped by listening to and reading the teaching of John Main on meditation. His teaching inspired and nourished me in the wobbly stages, and has continued to keep me steady on the path. This book is my attempt to distil his teaching and present it in a thematic form which may be helpful to anyone who wishes to tread the journey with the authoritative and yet gentle guidance of a master of prayer for our challenging times.

    Peter Ng
    President
    World Community for Christian Meditation, (Singapore)

Peter Ng has been meditating in the Christian tradition since 1988. He is a trustee of The World Community for Christian Meditation (WCCM) and also a member of its Guiding Board.

Peter is Chief Investment Officer and Board Director of the Government of Singapore Investment Corporation where he leads a team of investment professionals investing the nation's savings in global financial markets.

1 THE ESSENCE

The essence of meditation is learning to stand back and to allow God to come into the forefront of your life, to take that step away from self-centredness to God-centredness. The result is that we find our own place in the world, our relationships in the right order – our relationships with one another, our relationship with creation, and our relationship with God.

John Main

1.1	Fullness of Being
1.2	Leaving the Ego Behind
1.3	Discovering Our Potential
1.4	Ultimate Meaning
1.5	Expansion of Being
1.6	Re-linked to Our Centre

1.1 Fullness of Being

I thought it would be useful tonight if I try to summarize for you the essential elements of meditation.

I want to begin by reading to you from St Paul's letter to the Ephesians. He is reflecting upon the potential we all have for richer life, for a life rooted in the mystery of God. This is what he says:

> *I kneel in prayer to the Father, from whom every family in heaven and on earth takes its name, that out of the treasures of his glory he may grant you strength and power through his Spirit in your inner being, that through faith Christ may dwell in your hearts in love. With deep roots and firm foundations, may you be strong to grasp, with all God's people, what is the breadth and length and height and depth of the love of Christ, and to know it, though it is beyond knowledge. So may you attain to fullness of being, the fullness of God himself.* (Eph 3:14-19)

Now, that is a marvellous description of the destiny that each of us has, as Christians, as humans. Our destiny is to come to fullness of being, the fullness of God himself. In other words, each of us is summoned to an unlimited, infinite, development as we leave the narrowness of our own ego behind, and enter into the mystery of God.

Jesus has told us that his Spirit is to be found in our hearts. Meditating is uncovering this truth, this reality, deep within ourselves. The spirit that we are invited to discover in our hearts is the power source that enriches every part of our life. The spirit is the Spirit of life and the Spirit of love. The call of Christians is not to be half-alive, which means being half-dead, but to be fully alive,

alive with this power and energy that St Paul speaks of that is continually flowing in our hearts, if only we will undertake the discipline to make our way to it, day by day.

The way of meditation is simplicity itself. We simply have to begin, and to continue. It is essential to tread the path, to be on the way, each day of our lives.

When we meditate together in a few moments, each of us must sit still. That sitting still is of great importance. We place our body on this cushion, or in this chair, and we leave it there, totally devoted to the work of meditation. This is the first step away from egoism, away from concern with ourselves, opening our consciousness to what is beyond, to the infinite reality that expands our spirit into generous love. So we sit still.

Then, closing our eyes gently, we begin to recite our word, our mantra. The mantra I suggest you take is the Aramaic word *maranatha*. To meditate, all we have to do is to say the word from the beginning to the end. Ma-ra-na-tha. Don't think about it. Do not think about yourself. Do not wonder, "Is this a complete waste of time? Is this going to do me any good? What am I going to get out of this?" All those thoughts must fall away, must be abandoned. Meditation is bringing us to a state of undivided consciousness where we become one with the One who is one.

The call, the destiny, that you hear in St Paul that each of us has, is not a call just to enter into a *bit* of spiritual richness, but to enter fully and utterly without reserve, without counting the cost, entering into the truth that enables each of us to be fully human, fully confident – confident to love and to be loved. We must remember that we are not talking about some mysterious, esoteric doctrine. This call, this destiny, is within the reach of each one of us. All we have to do is commit ourselves to the journey, to the practice.

And the practice is – don't let anything mislead you on this – to say the word from the beginning to the end with growing fidelity. This truth is not only accessible to us, it is the ground on which all reality stands. To come to this reality we have to learn to be simple, to be still, to be silent, and to be attentive, attentive to what is – the supreme reality of God's presence, his love, within our own heart. So we must learn to stop thinking about ourselves. We must learn to *be*, to be in the presence of God, in the presence of the One who is, and who is the ground of our being. We need have no fear as we set out, as we leave self behind and set out to meet the other. We need have no fear. The spirit in our heart, the spirit that we open to in meditation, is the Spirit of compassion, of gentleness, of forgiveness, of total acceptance, the Spirit of love.

For our lives to be fully human we must encounter that Spirit of love within ourselves. This is not a journey just for spiritual experts. It is a journey for everyone who would live their lives to the full.

1.2 Leaving the Ego Behind

What is the essence of meditation? What is it really about?

It's learning to stand back and to allow God to come into the forefront of your life. So often in our experience, we find that *we* are the centre of our world. So many of us see reality revolving around us. We think quite naturally of situations and of people primarily in terms of "how is this going to affect me?" Now that's all right as far as it goes. But if we really imagine that we *are* at the centre of the world, then we are never going to see any situation, or any person, or ourselves, as we really are. Because, of course, we are not at the centre of the world. God is at the centre.

Now, meditation is trying to take that step away from self-centredness to God-centredness. The result is that we find our own place in the world. We find where we should be. We find our relationships in the right order – our relationships with one another, our relationship with creation, and our relationship with God. What we discover, and what is very important for each of us to discover, is that we do have an essential place in God's plan, each of us responding uniquely to the unique gift of our own creation. Perhaps that is the most important thing for people in our society to discover: their own dignity, their own unique gift, the gift of their own creation.

How can we set about this? Meditation is a discipline, and it is the discipline of learning to stand back, learning to focus our attention or, perhaps even better, focus our whole being on God. We have to begin somewhere. We have to begin with ourselves. We have to begin by learning to be silent ourselves. We have to really begin by learning to *be*, to be ourselves, not to be as it were defining ourselves by some activity, whether that activity is some work or some thinking process, but simply to be.

THE ESSENCE

Now this is the purpose of the practice and the art of meditation in learning to say our word, our mantra. To meditate, what we have to learn to do is to sit down, to be still, to be as still as possible physically, and then to begin to recite in our heart, in our mind, in our being, our word or our mantra. The word I recommend you to recite is the word *maranatha*. That's four equally-stressed syllables. You sound those syllables interiorly, silently, without moving your lips. As you sound them, you listen to them: ma-ra-na-tha.

The purpose of sounding them, the purpose of saying or sounding your mantra, is that that becomes the focus of your attention, of your concentration. You are not thinking about anything. You are not, as it were, pursuing any insights that are coming to you, any thoughts that are coming to you. You leave those. You let them, as it were, fall away. What you do is come to a greater and greater silence, where the only sound in your mind is the word, the mantra.

You have to learn, and the recitation of the mantra will teach you this, to be patient, to be extremely patient. You have to learn to be humble. In meditating, we are not seeking, as it were, to possess God. We are not seeking to come to some profound insights about God. We are seeking simply to be the person we are called to be. We are seeking simply to accept as fully as possible, and to respond to as fully as possible, the gift of our own creation. To do that, we have to learn to be still, to be silent, to be truly humble.

You are all familiar with the word 'egoism'. The word 'ego' is used a great deal in modern parlance or jargon. Basically, in meditation, we are leaving the ego behind. We are not trying to see with the ego, as it were, but we are trying to be ourself, our true self. The curious paradox is that, once we give up trying to see, once we give up trying to possess, we see all and all things are ours.

When you are beginning, you need to understand the simplicity of it. The simplicity is just this: that every morning and every evening, you give yourself the opportunity to be, to be in utter simplicity, to be in humility, not asking yourself, "What is happening to me now?" not trying to analyse yourself, "Am I enjoying this? Am I getting anything out of this?" During this time of being, you put your self-reflective ego entirely aside. And this you do every morning and every evening. And during the time of your meditation, just say your word, from the beginning to the end: ma-ra-na-tha. That's how to begin.

You have to begin on faith. There is no way that you can, as it were, evaluate what is happening when you begin. You have to begin in faith. But beginning will lead you into faith. You can't, as it were, have a stab at meditating – you say your word for three minutes and then stop to see how you are getting on. You have to learn, and you require patience to learn, to say your word from the beginning to the end, every day.

Where does this tie in, in Christian terms? In Christian terms, we know that God has sent his Spirit to dwell in our hearts. In other words, his being is within us, and meditating is simply being open to his being. Listen to St Paul writing to the Corinthians:

> *For the same God who said, 'Out of darkness, let light shine', has caused his light to shine within us, to give us the light of revelation – the revelation of the glory of God in the face of Jesus Christ.* (2 Cor 4:6)

That light and that glory are to be found in our hearts if only we will learn to be still, to be silent, to be humble. That is the exact purpose of the mantra – to lead us to that silence, stillness and humility.

1.3 Discovering Our Potential

The basic thing that we learn from meditation, from our own experience, is that God is Spirit. He is the breath of life. He is presence, and he is present deep within our being, in our hearts. What we discover, if only we persevere, is that in the power of his Spirit each one of us is regenerated, renewed, re-created, so that we do become a new creation in him. "I have poured out my Spirit upon this people", said the prophet Ezekiel. And the Spirit is the presence of power, the power of love.

Meditation teaches us that this is the foundational wisdom on which to build life and true religion. What we discover is that we can only live our lives fully if we are always open to this mysterious presence of the Spirit, and always open to the presence more profoundly. That is the pilgrimage we enter every time we sit down to meditate. We open our minds, our hearts, our consciousness to the ultimate reality that is, that is now, that is here. By being open to the mystery, to this reality, we are taken out of ourselves, beyond ourselves, into this absolute mystery which is God.

This is the mystery: the Kingdom of Heaven. And the Kingdom of Heaven is *now*. It is established by Jesus. In his own words: "The Kingdom of God is upon you; repent and believe the gospel." (Mark 1:15) To repent means simply to turn in the direction of God. Repenting is turning not so much away from ourselves but beyond ourselves. This means not rejecting ourselves, but finding, discovering our marvellous potential as we come into full harmony with God. That is the positive basis of Christianity. For a Christian, the important thing is not self, nor is it sin. The important thing is God and love and, as far as we are concerned, growth in that love. Growth in openness to his love for us and growth in our response in returning that love.

"Repent and believe the gospel." Believing the gospel simply means openness to our potential, the potential that each one of us possesses in the extraordinary plan of salvation. This is what Jesus reveals to each of us in our hearts as we undertake the journey of silence, and of absolute commitment to silence and to openness, every morning and every evening. What he reveals is that we are created for love, for freedom, for meaning, for fulfilment; and we realize it all by entering the mystery of the Kingdom that is upon us. That mystery is now unfolded by the generous gift of Christ. The Kingdom is established.

Remember the practicalities. Learn to be silent and to love silence. When we meditate we don't look for messages, or signs, or phenomena. Each of us must learn to be humble, patient, and faithful. We must learn to be still. We must learn to empty our heart of everything that is not God, for he requires all the room that our heart can offer. We learn that purity of heart by saying our mantra with absolute fidelity. The mystery is absolute truth, absolute love, and our response too must be absolute.

Listen to St Paul writing to the Corinthians:

> *As for me, brethren, when I came to you, I declared God's hidden secret without display of fine words or wisdom... I came before you weak as I was then... The word I spoke, the gospel I proclaimed, did not sway you with subtle arguments; it carried conviction by spiritual power, so that your faith might be built not upon human wisdom but upon the power of God.* (1 Cor 2:1, 3-5)

Let us now, in our meditation, prepare our hearts to be open to that power.

1.4 Ultimate Meaning

Why do we meditate? None of us, I suppose, would meditate unless it had occurred to us that there was more to life and to living than just being producers or consumers. All of us know that we can't find any enduring or ultimate meaning in just producing or just consuming. So we seek that ultimate meaning. We come to meditation because an unerring instinct tells us that, just as we can't find any ultimate satisfaction in consuming or producing, so we cannot find ultimate meaning simply outside of ourselves. We have to begin with ourselves.

In our society, there are a lot of people who, faced with the problem of being, living, and meaning, seek refuge in oblivion. You know the expression 'being stoned out of your mind'. And Marx, one of the most formative influences on the society in which we live, saw religion as being the opium of the people. There is a sense in which we can turn to religion as to anaesthesia, to be comforted or maybe to be put into a state of unconsciousness.

But Christian meditation has nothing to do with anaesthesia. Meditation is the way to illumination, to light and to life. Christ's message is one of vitalization and illumination: enlightenment. The way to this is the way of single-mindedness, not being distracted by things that are passing away but by being ever more deeply committed to what is enduring, to what is eternal.

Our own spirit is enduring. Our own spirit is eternal in God. That is all right as an intellectual insight, or even as a religious insight or a religious conviction. But the call of Christianity is the call of every truly spiritual doctrine. The call is to be open yourself to your own eternal spirit, to be open to your own rootedness in the Eternal, to start to tread the way, the pilgrimage to fullness of light and fullness of meaning. Now what is the way?

The way is the way of poverty, of simplicity. Let me remind you again of the way of meditation. Sit down and sit still, close your eyes, and begin to say your word *maranatha*. Say the word deliberately yet relaxedly; say it faithfully and yet serenely. Four syllables, all equally stressed: ma-ra-na-tha.

We say the word because the pilgrimage is a pilgrimage beyond ourselves, beyond our own limitations. To go beyond ourselves, we must transcend thought and imagination. The word is the way, the vehicle that carries us forward. The challenge of meditation is to undertake the discipline of saying the word, and continuing to say it, while learning to be patient, learning to wait, and learning that the way forward is the way to our own centre. The way to riches is the way of poverty. The way to enlightenment is the way of darkness. We have to go through with ever greater discipline, with ever greater faithfulness.

But understand this: The way is simple; it is not complicated. The way is sure. All that is required is the daily return to it, not with demands, not with any materialistic measuring of success. Just simple faithfulness, simple poverty of spirit; every morning and every evening devoting your time, not to what is passing, but to what is enduring – your own spirit alive and full of light in God.

1.5 Expansion of Being

We meditate because we understand that the human spirit was created for an infinite expansion of being. The whole thrust of the New Testament and of the Christian revelation is that every man and woman alive is made, is created, for this very growth, depth, maturity, and union with God.

One of the influences that we are all subject to is that of advertising. Modern advertising is always concerned with what is new, with novelty. So, for much of our experience of life, of reality, we tend to be concerned about what is new, what is the latest. In the end, instead of seeing our life as a whole and as a process of growth, of maturity, and of increasing depth, we simply move from one thing to another. We lose the sense of the connection between events, and our lives can so easily become distracted. The novelties are the distractions, one following the other. As we know too, if we do live our lives just moving from one novelty to another, very quickly we find a sort of dullness setting in. Nothing seems to satisfy us if we are just concerned with things that are outside of ourselves.

Now the way of meditation is an attempt to live your life and to understand your life no longer in terms of always finding some novelty. We seek an understanding infinitely greater than that, coming to an understanding that your life, every moment of it, is always new, not just a passing novelty. You discover that in every moment you are, as it were, springing from the creative hand of God. You will then soon discover that life is always marvellously fresh, continually exciting, because it is always expanding. Your sights are always expanding into infinity, not contracting into this or that passing object of satisfaction. That's why a person meditates.

Now what must we do? How do we set out on this? If you want to meditate, the first thing you require is to be serious about it. Not solemn, but serious. To see this as an invitation, as a possibility, that will lead you to the deepest personal actualization of your potential. If you want to learn to meditate, you must put aside the time for it every day of your life. Ideally, you should find a time every morning and every evening. The daily discipline is of immense importance. You can't just, as it were, admire the spiritual realities from a distance. You must enter in. You must taste and see. The time I recommend you to spend in meditation is a minimum of twenty minutes, and the optimum time is half an hour, every morning and every evening.

1.6 Re-linked to Our Centre

I want to try and describe to you this evening what meditation is really about. Meditation is simply a way of coming to your own centre, and remaining in your centre awake, alive, and still. The great problem with the lives of so many of us is that we live at an incredibly shallow level. By meditating, we seek to find our way to the depths of our own being.

The word 'meditation' comes from the Latin *meditare* which suggests *stare in medio* – to remain in the centre. The word 'contemplation' is the same. The word contemplation does not mean looking at anything – God or anyone else. Contemplation is 'being in the temple' with God. The temple is your own heart, the depths of your own being.

We meditate leaving the shallow levels of our life behind, and entering into something that is profound. In meditating, we leave behind the passing, ephemeral things of life and enter into what is eternal. The ultimate goal of all religion is a re-linking, and the re-linking is a re-linking with our own centre. That's the purpose of all religion, that we are re-linked to our own centre.

In the Christian revelation, in our heart, in the depths of our own spirit, dwells the Spirit of God. The truth we discover from our own experience, if only we will tread the pilgrimage, is that there is only one centre and that that centre is everywhere.

What I think each one of us has to discover from our own experience is that this is the first responsibility of our lives. It is the first responsibility of every life that would be fully human: to return to our own centre, and to live out of the depths of our own profound capacity. We discover that being reconnected with our own centre reconnects us with every centre. The truly spiritual man or woman learns to live in harmony with themselves, and to live in harmony with the whole of creation.

What we can say is: To be in one's own centre is to be in God. In the words of Jesus, "The Kingdom of Heaven is within you." (Luke 17:21) We must remember that this kingdom is not a place, but an experience. The experience is the experience of the reality of the power of God. In the Christian vision, it is knowing that that power is the power of love.

St John of the Cross put it this way: "God is the centre of my soul." At the centre we experience silence, stillness, and the peace that is beyond all understanding. The way to this is the way of the mantra.

Let me be very practical. In meditating, we seek to enter into an ever more profound simplicity. The way is the way of unlearning. The way is the way of dispossession. The way is the way of simplicity. We unlearn and we dispossess ourselves by turning aside from all our own words and thoughts and staying solely with the mantra. That is what takes us to the depths.

What all of us must understand is this. You can't just do a *bit* of meditation. If you want to meditate, then you have to place it in a central place in your life. You have to make sure that everything in your life is in harmony with the harmony you find in your own spirit. You cannot live, as it were, a double life and be a harmonious integrated person on your way to depth, to enlightenment and to profound vitalization. You have to be a simple person. You have to be a person who is living the oneness in your own life.

I want to end by reading to you from the first letter of St Peter. This is something all of us have to listen to carefully. The problem for people in our own time in learning to meditate is to have a sufficient grasp of their own potentiality as well as a sufficient belief that they really can live out of profounder depths than the shallowness of every day. These words of St Peter are a call to us to recognize who we are, to recognize our own dignity, to recognize the wonder of our own being, and to recognize above all else our own lovableness.

So come to him, our living Stone – the stone rejected by men but choice and precious in the sight of God. Come to him and let yourselves be built, as living stones, into a spiritual temple; become a holy priesthood, to offer spiritual sacrifices through Jesus Christ. For ... you are a chosen race, a royal priesthood, a dedicated nation, and a people claimed by God for his own, to proclaim the triumphs of him who has called you out of darkness into his marvellous light. (1 Pet 2:4-5,9)

2 THE PRACTICE

Meditation is very, very simple. Don't complicate it... Meditation is perfect stillness of body and spirit. In that stillness, we open our hearts to the eternal silence of God, to be swept out of ourselves, beyond ourselves, by the power of that silence.

John Main

2.1	How to Meditate
2.2	The Basic Doctrine
2.3	Times of Meditation
2.4	Distractions
2.5	Preparations to Meditate

2.1 How to Meditate

To meditate, you must learn to be still. Meditation is perfect stillness of body and spirit. The stillness of body, we achieve by sitting still. So when you begin to meditate, take a couple of moments to assume a comfortable posture. The only essential rule is to have your spine as upright as possible. And so the first thing to learn is to sit completely still. Your eyes should be lightly closed.

Then the stillness of spirit. The way to that stillness is to say silently, in the depth of your spirit, a word or a short phrase, to repeat that word over and over again. The word I recommend you to use is the Aramaic word *maranatha*. Say it in four equally-stressed syllables: ma-ra-na-tha. Say it silently; don't move your lips but recite it interiorly. Recite your word from beginning to end. Let go of your thoughts, of your ideas, of your imagination. Don't think. Don't use any words other than your one word. Just sound, say, the word in the depth of your spirit, and listen to it. Concentrate upon it with all your attention: ma-ra-na-tha. That's all you have to do.

2.2 The Basic Doctrine

The essence of meditating is learning to recite, from the beginning until the end of your meditation, a word that is called in some traditions a mantra. The essential teaching of meditation is contained in the three words: Say your mantra.

It's very difficult, for people starting, to believe that there could be anything very significant in sitting still, closing your eyes lightly, and just reciting a word. You have to take that on faith when you begin.

The word that I recommend you to recite is the Aramaic word *maranatha* – four equally-stressed syllables. Don't bother about what it means, and certainly don't think about what it means. Don't think about God; don't think about anything. Say your word, recite it, and listen to it.

I first started to meditate about thirty years ago. I suppose that I was as crass as anyone of my age, because I was always saying to the man who taught me: "How long is this going to take? I can't sit around here saying this word forever, you know." He would look at me with a rather pained look, and either he would just look straight through me, or else he would say: "Say your mantra." In the last thirty years, I have been more and more struck by the extraordinary wisdom of his teaching.

Say your mantra. That is the first thing to understand. It may take you five or ten years to understand that – to say your mantra from the beginning to the end of your meditation, without ceasing. We must learn to be disciplined, and we must learn to leave our thoughts and imagination entirely behind. The mantra, the faithful recitation of the mantra, is the way. As I say, it has taken me a good part of thirty years to understand the importance of that.

Meditating is sometimes called the prayer of faith. In it we seek to leave self behind and to be open to the powerful personal presence of Christ in our hearts. The word that we say, our mantra, is like the sacrament, the outward sign of our faith in his presence.

However peaceful you are feeling, recite it. However drowsy you are feeling, recite it. However difficult it is for you, recite it. However much you are getting out of it, or however little you are getting out of it, recite your word.

If you can understand that, you've understood almost all there is to understand of the basic doctrine: Say your mantra from beginning to end.

2.3 Times of Meditation

If you want to learn to meditate, it's essential to meditate every day of your life; if you can, every morning and every evening. The optimum time for meditating is probably half an hour; the minimum time is twenty minutes. Anything less than that, you haven't really begun. So what I recommend you to do, when you are beginning, is to meditate for about twenty-five minutes and gradually put it up to thirty minutes.

The really important thing is the discipline of meditating. Choose a specific time, twenty, twenty-five or thirty minutes, and always meditate for that time. You have to be very practical about it. Find a way of measuring that time so that you are not glancing at your watch every five minutes saying, "Surely to God, it must be over by now."

People use all sorts of devices. Some people, for example, take a 45-minute cassette tape and 'record' on it a half-hour of silence, and at the end of the silence, put in some quiet music. So you press the button when you start to meditate, and when the music comes you know that your half-hour is up. Other people use a sort of kitchen cooking timer.

When we are starting, the temptation is, if things are going 'well' and you are approaching cloud nine, to prolong the meditation. Or, if things are going 'badly', you say, "Well, this is a total waste of time; might as well cut this out and go and cut the lawn or something." The important thing is to stick at it, whether it is going well or going badly or however it is going. There is only one way for it to go, and that is that you say your mantra from beginning to end.

The best time is probably early in the morning, before breakfast, and when you are at your freshest. Perhaps a cold shower too might be part of the prescription. In the evening, probably the best time is before your evening meal. That isn't always very possible for everybody, if you are coming home from work and your meal is ready. It depends very much on the circumstances of your life. Those are probably the optimum times. But what is of supreme importance is that you do meditate every morning and every evening. If you can, it's good to build in a regular routine. It's not possible in everyone's life to do that. But the general rules for the times of meditation are: If you can, meditate first thing in the morning, and then always meditate before a meal rather than after it. Probably the optimum times for meditating are the early morning and early evening. Now everyone has their own series of responsibilities that they have to respond to during the day, so you have to do the best you can. Sometimes, the only time you can meditate is in the early afternoon, perhaps sometimes in the later evening. But, if you can choose the same time and, if possible, the same place, that is probably the best. But all of us have to do the best we can in the circumstances of our lives.

Ideally, it is useful to meditate in a very quiet place so that you can be as recollected as possible. But if your next-door neighbour starts using a steam hammer and that recollection is lost, it is much preferable to keep on meditating rather than to say, "Well, I haven't got the ideal circumstances, therefore I'll give up." For example, when I was coming home from Ireland last week on the plane, I decided that the time had come to meditate. The air hostess decided that it was a good time to have a chat with a passenger who seemed to be looking rather lonely or rather quiet. She came and sat down beside me, so I chatted with her for a while. It was on Aer Lingus, Irish International Airlines. She was rather more than usually loquacious. It took me some time before I could politely return to my meditation. You have to do the best that you can in the circumstances.

The really critical thing is to put in those two meditations. A priest friend of mine started to meditate about six years ago. He said that when he started, he listened to what I had to say and said,

"Well, you know, this guy is a monk, nothing to do all day, sitting around. It's very easy for him to meditate twice a day, but I'm a busy parish priest. Therefore, I will read his signal: for me, once a day." And so, he said, for about a year, he meditated once a day. Then he said, "You know, this is not working." He came to me to complain about it. And I said, "Well, it's extraordinary. You meditate every morning and every evening, do you?" He said, "No, no, just the morning." So I said, "Well, you meditate in the evening as well and then we'll listen to the complaints." And he did. He said he couldn't describe to me the qualitative difference, once he began his day and, as it were, prepared for his day out of that peace and inner rootedness in his essential being. And then bringing the whole day together at the end, as it were, gathering all the strands into the same essential reality. He said the qualitative difference was astonishing to him. He said, "You know, I'll meditate every day, twice a day, for the rest of my life now, if I possibly can." I would always advise you not to give up, even though you are tired, to do your best to put in the evening meditation.

The morning time of meditation is to set the tone for your day, to set out onto your daily pilgrimage knowing who you are, setting out on it prepared by your meditation. Then your evening meditation is to bring together all the various strands of the day's activities, and unify them by your own concentration. So you must understand that the daily discipline is of immense importance.

2.4 Distractions

As we start to meditate, we discover that we are full of distractions.

We sit down, we sit upright, we breathe calmly, and we close our eyes and begin to say our mantra, our word. And then, our thoughts begin to take over. The thoughts are usually quite insidious, because it can often be: "I wonder would I be able to say my mantra better if I was sitting not in the half lotus but the full lotus. Now, how could I learn to sit in the full lotus?" Ten minutes later, you think of what you are going to have for dinner or something, and maybe twenty minutes later, you can get back to saying the mantra again.

What should you do when you begin to meditate and distracting thoughts come into your mind? The advice that the tradition has to give us is to ignore the distractions and say your word, and keep saying your word. Don't waste any energy in trying to furrow your brow and say, "I will not think of what I am going to have for dinner", or "who I'm going to see today", or "where I'm going tomorrow", or whatever the distraction may be. Don't try to use any energy to dispel the distraction. Simply ignore it, and the way to ignore it is to say your word. In other words, when you meditate, your energy must be channelled in a single course, and the way of that course is your word.

What you have to learn is that the important thing is to say the mantra from the beginning to the end. When you find you have strayed from it, return to it immediately, not violently but gently.

You must learn to let those distractions just fall away from your mind, and return to the mantra. You will find as you go on that you can be saying your mantra at one level and there is one level of thoughts going on below, another on top, another on the side, another on the other side. Ignore them all. Say your mantra.

It's as though, when we start to meditate, we are caught in some storm, the storm of distraction. There are flashes of lightning going on everywhere; there are howling gales going on all around us. The mantra is just like a beacon taking us through, and we must keep our attention on it. If we take our attention off the mantra, we are lost.

There are different levels of distraction. There is the distraction that comes just from the immediacy of our lives: the last TV programme we were watching, advertising, newspapers, conversations we were just having. We must let all that go as we listen to the mantra. Then there are the personal distractions: the problems of our relationships in our family, our career, our friends, the loneliness we may feel. All these, too, we must let go as we come into the presence, the presence of the One who is, who is Love. Then there are the spiritual distractions: wondering about our spiritual progress, comparing our experience over someone else's, analysing the state we are in, whatever. All those distractions, we must let go. We let go of them by being really faithful to our mantra. If you find that you are thinking about the TV programme, or some problem in your family, or about your spiritual progress, drop it immediately and return to the mantra. Ma-ra-na-tha.

One of the things that all of us find as we tread our path of meditation with simplicity and with humility is that there will be certain things in our lives that have to change. For example, I should think it would be very difficult to meditate if you spend three or four hours a day watching television. A great enemy of all prayer and all recollection is a plethora of images in our minds. You will all discover, and I am sure you are already discovering from your own experience, that it is foolishness to add indiscriminately to this plethora of images.

The greatest of all distractions is self-consciousness. This arises because of the tendency we all have to look at ourselves. But, in meditating, we look beyond ourselves to God. The mantra expands our vision beyond ourselves. All those first types of distractions were external. Self-consciousness is internal. The power of meditation is that it tackles the source of all distraction at the root, and the root is self-consciousness. In meditating, we learn to stop thinking about ourselves, to go on a journey looking ahead and staying on the journey. The guarantee of staying on the journey is that we say our mantra, keep saying our mantra and constantly returning to it.

Don't be worried by your distractions. Don't rate yourself for success. Say your mantra and be content to say it. And continue to say it. In the face of distraction, don't use any energy to try to dispel the distraction. Use all your energy to say your mantra, with absolute gentleness but absolute fidelity.

2.5 Preparations to Meditate

The purpose of meditating is that we can learn to live our lives as fully as possible in the presence of God. Learning to live in his presence means also being energized with his energy. As we know from the gospel, his energy is love. Learning to meditate is learning constantly to be in this presence and constantly to live out of that presence.

To learn anything, we have to learn to listen. We have to learn the humility to listen, and then to begin the simple tasks involved in learning. If you want to learn to play a musical instrument, you have to learn to play the scales. If you want to learn a language, you have to learn the elementary grammar. You have to be content to learn that, because without the foundation of that simple learning no progress is possible.

In learning to meditate, perhaps the first thing we have to learn is to sit well, to sit with a good posture. The essential rule of posture is that our spine is upright. The essential rule of our sitting is that we sit still. So one of the first things we must learn is the physical stillness of meditation. We sit still, not just so as to get the body out of the way, but so that body and spirit can both be harmoniously involved, unified, in our meditation. Meditation is a complete unity of body and spirit, still and present to God.

Now we have to prepare ourselves to meditate. The first preparation is the goodness each of us must practise in our everyday living. That's of great importance: that we learn to prepare ourselves by simple kindness, forgiveness, simple goodness.

Then, the immediate preparation is the quiet of the place we choose to meditate and the quietness of our body as we prepare for the inner quietness of the spirit, leading us to that total attentiveness of body and spirit.

It's good, I think, to come to your meditation purified, to wash at least your face and hands, so that you can wash away the dust of the day or the drowsiness of the night. This washing prepares the body to be alert for the purity of meditation.

Then we prepare our spirit by regular, calm, deep breathing. This sets the scene for the serious work that we are entering into. Remember, meditation is entering into the presence of the One who is. It is in his presence, the presence of the One who is, that each of us learns to *be*, to be the person we are called to be. To meditate we must pass beyond all images, above all, the image that we have of ourselves. So when we begin to meditate, we divest ourselves of all our masks. We, as it were, set them down on the ground beside us, and we begin to become the real person we are, in absolute simplicity. Then we begin to say our mantra: ma-ra-na-tha. Remember, we are saying our mantra not to impress anyone or to create any further image of ourselves, a spiritual image. We are saying our mantra in order to leave all images, all words, behind so that we can be in utter simplicity.

3 THE THEOLOGY

The theology is that THE *prayer is the prayer of Jesus.... We have to stand back sufficiently enough to allow his prayer full power within us.*

John Main

3.1	The Theology of Prayer
3.2	Only One Prayer
3.3	Beyond All Concepts of God
3.4	To Lose Ourselves in Christ
3.5	God's Mysterious Presence within Us
3.6	The Birth of Christ in Our Hearts
3.7	Transformation of Human Consciousness
3.8	Death and Resurrection

3.1 The Theology of Prayer

This evening, I want to put before you what is the essential theology of prayer.

We know from the doctrine of the indwelling of the Holy Spirit that the fullness of God is to be found in our own hearts. We know that the full life of the Trinity is lived in our hearts. This means that Jesus Christ dwells in our hearts. His human consciousness is to be found within each one of us. The journey of prayer is simply to find the way to open our human consciousness to his human consciousness.

The reason why in the Christian tradition we meditate is that we believe that Jesus has sent his Spirit to dwell in our hearts. In other words, the Spirit of God, the Spirit of the Creator of the universe, dwells in our hearts, and in silence is loving to all. In the Christian tradition, meditating is simply being open to this Spirit of Love, the Spirit of God.

Listen to St Paul writing to the Colossians:

Therefore since Jesus was delivered to you as Christ and Lord, live your lives in union with him. Be rooted in him; be built in him... For it is in Christ that the complete being of the Godhead dwells embodied; and in him, you have been brought to completion. (Col 2:6-7, 9)

This is what the essential message of Christianity is about, that our call and our potential is to enter into the life of God through Jesus, through his Spirit present in our hearts.

We do this, not by analysing God or analysing Jesus, not by thinking about God or thinking about Jesus, but by being silent and still, and in his presence opening our hearts to his love, and doing so in the steady rhythm of our daily meditation.

This is the wonder of the doctrine of the Incarnation because Jesus, being man and possessing a human consciousness, is our way to the Father, because it is possible for us to open our human consciousness to his. That is the marvel, the perfection, of the Christian revelation – that he is *the* Way, and he is the *only* Way. He is the universal Redeemer and the universal Sanctifier. He is so for us because his human consciousness is fully open to the Father in love. When in the silence of prayer, in the concentration of our meditation, we open our human consciousness to him, we go beyond him, to the Father. We go beyond him by his power of self-transcending love.

3.2 Only One Prayer

Listen to these words of Jesus:

May they all be one as thou, Father, art in me and I in thee; so also may they be in us, that the world may believe that thou dids't send me. The glory which thou gavest to me, I have given to them, that they may be one as we are one, I in them and thou in me. May they be perfectly one, and then the world will learn that thou dids't send me, and that thou dids't love them as thou dids't me.

Father, I desire that these men who are thy gift to me may be with me where I am, so that they may look upon my glory which thou has given me, because thou dids't love me before the world began. O righteous Father, although the world does not know thee, I know thee and these men know that thou dids't send me. I made thy name known to them and will make it known, so that the love thou hads't for me may be in them and I may be in them. (John 17:20-26)

As far as our tradition is concerned, there is only one prayer, and that is the prayer of Jesus. He is the universal mediator. There is no way to the Father except through Jesus.

The definition of prayer given by John Cassian's teacher, Evagrius, is the classical one: "Prayer is the raising of the mind and heart to God." The only way we can raise our minds and hearts to God is through Jesus. So his is the only prayer, and the only prayer for us is to open our hearts as fully as we can to his prayer. This process has been called in the tradition of the Church the prayer of faith, contemplative prayer, pure prayer – various names it has been known by. We call it meditation: being still in the centre of our being so that we may travel with Christ to the centre of the Trinity.

There are other forms of prayer. For example, we as monks spend quite a bit of time each day at liturgical prayer. All other forms of prayer lead us into this pure experience of God. So meditation is not in any sense exclusive. We are not saying to anyone, do not waste time saying the rosary, don't waste time saying your Breviary. What we are saying is: Enter into the pure stream of the prayer of Jesus. Launch yourself into that stream by any means you can find, whether it is the rosary, the Stations of the Cross, the Divine Office, or whatever.

What we say is: To enter into that stream of pure prayer, you must transcend yourself; you must leave yourself behind. Learning to say your mantra, and learning to discipline yourself to prayer every day, is the way the tradition gives us and the way our own experience gives us for journeying with Jesus, through Jesus, to the Father.

The theology is that *the* prayer is the prayer of Jesus. We have to stand back and allow his prayer, as it were, full power within us. As soon as you realize that the Way is the prayer of Jesus, that that is *the* Way, then your only challenge is to stand back sufficiently enough to allow his prayer to become supereminent.

What you are doing is, as it were, being launched into that prayer. It is very difficult to talk about it without images, but the prayer of Jesus is just like a rushing torrent flowing between Jesus and the Father. What we have to do is to plunge ourselves into that, and be swept along by it. It is a torrent of love, not a torrent of words. That is why we have to learn to be wholly silent. The mantra is simply bringing us deeper and deeper into that silence.

3.3 Beyond All Concepts of God

Perhaps the people who misunderstand about meditation more often than anyone else are religious and perhaps people we might describe as devout practising Christians. Time and again when I have been talking to such groups of people, they become almost scandalized at the idea of saying the mantra. They say, "Surely this would be to try to put God in a strait-jacket. Surely this would be to stifle all my own spontaneity." The principal reason for this misunderstanding is that so many people fail to understand the first principle in Christian prayer. The most important thing to remember is that there is only the prayer of Jesus. This is *the* prayer. The prayer of Jesus is the torrent of love and power flowing between Jesus and the Father, that is the Spirit.

This is the first thing for us to try to understand in Christian prayer, and of course we cannot understand it. This is the extraordinary thing about Christianity – although we can never understand it, we can experience this torrent of love flowing between Jesus and the Father. We can experience it through the human consciousness of Jesus. That is his great gift to us. Indeed that is our redemption. That is our salvation. Because, it is in his human consciousness that we are delivered from our own egoism and isolation, delivered from that into the mystery of God as we travel in that stream of love.

The great thing about the Christian revelation that we must enter into, and open our hearts to, is that Jesus himself does not ask us to rest in him, but to go beyond him to the Father. This is the essence of the Christian mystery: to transcend self into Jesus and, in Jesus, to transcend Jesus into the Father.

The theology of prayer is the theology of the Trinity. When we begin to see it in this experiential dimension, it is simply mind-boggling. The mind cannot contain the mystery, cannot hold it together in its being. That is why we must go beyond all concepts of God. We must, in other words, transcend the language, the insights, everything that could possibly limit God. We must know God with God's own self-knowledge; our knowledge is totally inadequate. The perfection of the human mind is as nothing compared to the wholly ineffable mystery. That is why we need to tread the path of simplicity. It is the simplicity of God, the simplicity of his oneness, that provides the greatest stumbling block for us. The mantra is the way over that stumbling block. The mantra, if you like, is like a sign or symbol of the oneness, the simplicity of God.

A question that constantly recurs is: "What are we actually doing when we are meditating? What place does it have in our Christian life in general?" When people begin meditating and they are told, "You must say your word from the beginning to the end, and you mustn't speak to God or think of God but you must say your word", they say, "But is this prayer? Is it Christian prayer at all? Or is it just some form of relaxation or some form of self-hypnosis?" Now, in the New Testament, you find that one of its recurring themes is that *the* prayer is the prayer of Jesus, and it is *his* prayer that we must learn to be part of, to enter. Saying the mantra, saying your word, is simply keeping a guard over your heart so that extraneous trivia cannot enter in, even the extraneous trivia of your own pious, holy, words and thoughts. Nothing must dilute that stream of prayer that is the love of Jesus for his Father. We must be wholly open to that. The mantra is like a watchdog, guarding your heart. That is why you must learn to say it from the beginning to the end of your meditation.

My advice to you is to see your times of meditation not as times that are at your disposition at all. See your meditation, your prayer, not as *your* prayer but as the prayer of Jesus. As long as we think self-importantly about *my* meditation, or *my* prayer, we have not really started on the pilgrimage. The time is his, the prayer is his.

The miracle is that his prayer is our prayer, and it is simplicity that brings us to this total confidence and unshakeable confidence in the Father, which the Gospel describes as hope. We approach meditation with no hesitation, but with a childlike sense of availability to God.

The requirement is total selflessness, a total abandoning of all our thoughts, imagination, insight, and above all abandoning of our own prayers and an openness to the prayer of Jesus in our heart.

Prayer is the life of the Spirit of Jesus within our human heart. We are praying when we are awakening to the presence of this Spirit in our heart.

3.4 To Lose Ourselves in Christ

This is from the Gospel of Matthew:

No man is worthy of me who does not take up his cross and walk in my footsteps. By gaining his life, a man will lose it; by losing his life for my sake, he will gain it. (Matt 10:38-39)

A little later in the same Gospel:

Jesus then said to his disciples, 'If anyone wishes to be a follower of mine, he must leave self behind; he must take up his cross and come with me. Whoever cares for his own safety is lost, but if a man will let himself be lost for my sake, he will find his true self. What will a man gain by winning the whole world, at the cost of his own true self? Or what can a man give that will buy that self back?' (Matt 16:24-26)

I think all of us have read the Gospel, and all of us who have tried to open our hearts to the call of Jesus, can sense the truth in those words. The paradox that Jesus puts before us is that to find our life we must lose it. That paradox, we know at a deep level of our being, is true.

The challenge that each one of us faces is this: How are we going to lose our life, to lay down our life, so that we can follow Jesus, not just at the limit of our life but at the centre, not just at the periphery but at the depth of our own being?

From the beginning of the time when people have listened to Jesus and tried to respond to him, his disciples knew the way of prayer. He himself was the great example. As we know from the Gospels, he often withdrew from his disciples to be alone with his Father. That is exactly the invitation that we have – to leave the surface, to leave the periphery, and at the centre to be at one with Jesus, to be with him in the Father.

All of us who are here tonight have come from different starting places, and all of us come with our own personal history, but all of us have one aim: to find Jesus and to find ourselves in him. The way of prayer that we as monks follow is the way of meditation. That is, each time we sit down to pray, we try to lose ourselves in Christ and find our true self in him.

Prayer is communion, oneness. In prayer, the way we travel is to become wholly absorbed in Jesus and to travel with him in his return to the Father. It is a way of simplicity. You have to learn to be content to say your word. It is a way of discipline. You have to learn to leave behind your own thoughts, your own insights. During meditation, very often, you may have some thought, some insight that might seem very profound, very religious, very significant. But, meditating is the way of poverty. In the time of your meditation, you surrender those thoughts, those insights, into the hands of God. You learn to be childlike, to be as simple as a child, to say your word, and to be content in saying it.

Let us end with a prayer.

> *Heavenly Father, we know that we must lose our lives in order that we may find them. We know that we must enter fully into the mystery of your Divine Life. Strengthen us, give us courage. Root your mantra in our minds, in our hearts, in the core of our being, so that we may become truly poor in spirit, that we may grow fully open to your gift of life and fullness.*

3.5 God's Mysterious Presence within Us

The central reality of our Christian faith is the sending of the Spirit by Jesus. Our faith is a living faith because the living Spirit of God dwells within us, giving new life to our mortal bodies.

Just listen to Chapter 5 of Paul's letter to the Romans; he is talking about what God has accomplished in the person of his son Jesus:

> *Therefore, now that we have been justified through faith, let us continue at peace with God through our Lord Jesus Christ, through whom we have been allowed to enter the sphere of God's grace, where we now stand. Let us exult in the hope of the divine splendour that is to be ours... because God's love has flooded our inmost heart through the Holy Spirit he has given us.* (Rom 5:1-5)

Just think about this language for a moment, and consider the quite staggering claim it is making: "We have been allowed to enter the sphere of God's grace, where we now stand." "God's love has flooded our inmost heart through the Holy Spirit he has given us."

All Christian prayer is basically the experience of being filled with the Spirit. In Romans 8, Paul puts it this way:

> *We do not even know how to pray, but through our inarticulate groans the Spirit himself is pleading for us, and God who searches our inmost being knows what the Spirit means.* (Rom 8:26-7)

In meditation, our way forward to this growing awareness of the Spirit praying within us is simply in our deepening fidelity to the saying of the mantra. It is the faithful repetition of our word that integrates our whole being. It does so because it brings us to the silence, the concentration, the necessary level of consciousness that enables us to open our mind and heart to the work of the love of God in the depths of our being.

In meditation, we do not seek to think about God. Nor do we seek to think about his Son, Jesus. Nor do we seek to think about the Holy Spirit. In meditation, we are trying to do something immeasurably greater. By turning aside from everything that is passing, we seek not just to think about God, but to *be* with God, to experience him as the ground of our being. It is one thing to know that Jesus is the revelation of the Father, that Jesus is our Way to the Father, but quite another to experience the presence of Jesus within us, to experience the real power of his Spirit within us, and in that experience to be brought into the presence of his Father and our Father.

Now this is our aim in Christian meditation: to allow God's mysterious and silent presence within us to become more and more not only a reality, but *the* reality in our lives; that reality which gives meaning, shape and purpose to everything we do, to everything we are.

Let us end with a spoken prayer.

Heavenly Father, open my heart to the silent presence of the Spirit of your Son. Lead me into that mysterious silence where your Love is revealed to all who call. Maranatha. Ma-ra-na-tha. Come Lord Jesus.

3.6 The Birth of Christ in Our Hearts

As we all are preparing for Christmas, I thought tonight I would try to reflect with you about the essential spiritual significance of the Incarnation. God became Man so that Man can become God. This is the constant conviction of the Eastern Churches. In the writing of the Greek Fathers, this theme continually comes through: God became man so that man can become God. In the Incarnation, God has touched our lives in Jesus. The great importance of the feast of Christmas is that it is the celebration of our humanity, redeemed.

What the Incarnation, the birth of Jesus, is about is the revelation of God. It is the revelation of his power, his wisdom, his love in the man Jesus. The Incarnation is like a pouring out of God on earth. As you know, in the life of Jesus, nothing is held back. The generosity of God is incarnated in the generosity of Jesus. In his lifetime, we see his availability to the crowds, his compassion for the sick, for the mourning. His utter selflessness, we know, comes to a climax in his death on the cross.

The great proclamation of the early Church is that he lives in our hearts. The German mystic Silesius, reflecting upon the feast of the Nativity, said that it may be that Jesus was born in Bethlehem, but that will be of no avail to us unless he is born in our hearts. That is the whole purpose of Christian meditation. Christ was born at Bethlehem, and that is a marvellous historical fact. But it is a fact that is completed, that was completed in the past. Now, he must be born in our hearts. Our hearts must be made ready for him. That is all meditation is – a readying of our heart for the birth of Christ. And it is because he is the infinite God that we must let go of everything else, so that there is space for him in our hearts.

The mystery is that when he is come to birth in our hearts, everything is come to birth with him. Our hearts are filled with all love, all compassion, all forgiveness. We know ourselves forgiven, loved and understood by the infinite God and by his Son, our brother. Meditation is our daily experience of leaving self behind to be open to God, in his Son Jesus, by the power of the Spirit.

Meditation is so important because meditation is itself an absolute commitment. It is a commitment to be open to Christ totally, utterly, by taking the attention off ourselves and putting it on him. And the way we do this is a simple way – by reciting our mantra.

This is an absolute commitment. Either you recite it or you do not. You can follow your own thoughts; you can make your own plans; you can analyse your own insights when you are meditating. But if you do, you will soon learn from your own experience that you remain in the closed system of self-consciousness. Reciting the mantra and continuing to recite it, is letting go of your own thoughts, fears, sadness and planning. Letting go releases us into the liberty and the infinity of God. This is what Jesus calls us to, to trust in him and follow him, not by half measures but in absolute measure. In his gentleness he gives us a way that leads us, by a steady progression, away from self into his infinite mystery. That way is the way of prayer, the way of meditation.

The way is the way of daily fidelity. Wherever we are on the path – whether we are just beginning and meditating twice every day for twenty minutes, or whether we have been on the path for some time and we meditate for thirty minutes or meditate three times a day – wherever we are, all that is required is that we give ourselves totally to our commitment. It seems, when we begin, that this is asking a lot. But the feast of Christmas reminds us that God in his gift to us does not just give us a lot; he gives us everything of himself, in Jesus. Somehow we must understand that, and we must understand it in the silence of our own heart.

And so when we meditate we, each of us, receive as fully as we can the gift of God in Jesus. To receive it, we require a generosity that is not less than the generosity of God. That is why we must say our mantra with the greatest attention we can, with the greatest love we can.

3.7 Transformation of Human Consciousness

It is our great fortune as monks to be able to stand aside from much of the hurly-burly and to have time to reflect and to consider the basic nature of the human condition. It is our conviction that the life, teaching, death and resurrection of Jesus have radically transformed the potential for the development of human consciousness. It is our conviction too that if we want to live our lives fully, then somehow or other, we must come to terms with this fact of the life and death and resurrection of Jesus, because his life, his teaching, and his death and resurrection, have placed new areas of experience within our reach. No longer are we cut off from the experience of God. We are invited to enter right into the heart of the divine mystery, and every one of us is invited.

It is also our conviction as monks that there is nothing to be gained merely by talking about all this. To talk about the transformation of consciousness arising from the life of Jesus will get us nowhere unless we actually take the practical steps to enter into this process of transformation. The one thing we have to share with you is that it is the practice of meditation that is of supreme importance.

What Jesus has done for us, in the language of the New Testament, is to send his Spirit to dwell in our hearts. His Spirit is open in love to God the Father. By our being open in love to the Spirit of Jesus, we are transported into the love of the Father too, with him and through him. In other words, our human consciousness, and that means the consciousness of everyone here, is summoned to an infinite expansion, infinite development. We are summoned to full maturity as human beings; and we can only come to that full maturity by being open to the human consciousness of Jesus. What Jesus has done, what he has achieved in his life, in effect, is to bring the divine within the ambiance of every man and woman alive.

The question however remains: How do we open our human consciousness to the human consciousness of Jesus? It is here that we turn to meditation. In meditation, we seek to disassemble the barriers that we have set up around ourselves, cutting us off from our consciousness of the presence of Jesus within our own hearts. In meditating, we start the process of dismantling the ego that attempts to place ourselves at the centre. We begin to understand that God is at the centre, and so our perspective changes. In the practice of meditation, we begin to learn what real humility is about: seeing ourselves in our proper place. Meditation also teaches us that we can reach God the Father through the human consciousness of Jesus. We discover by meditating in faith that Jesus is the bridge that takes us to the further shore. He is the ferry that takes us across the river of egoism and launches us into the river of divine love. Egoism leads to isolation. Meditation leads us through this isolation into the love of God.

Gradually, we come to realize that love is the basis of all reality, and that we are invited to live our lives fully in this love by our commitment to gentleness, to compassion, to understanding. The great fact of the experience of meditating is this: Once we do enter into the human consciousness of Jesus, we begin to see as he sees, to love as he loves, to understand as he understands, and to forgive as he forgives. Our angle of vision on the whole of creation is profoundly altered. Again remember the pre-eminence of the practice. It is necessary to meditate every day, every morning and every evening.

You may well ask: "How will this bring me to this compassion and forgiveness, to this love?" When you begin, you have to take that on faith. There is no way of answering that question except through the practice. Basically, the reason is this: What stops us from compassion, what stops us from recognizing the presence of Jesus in our heart as the presence of the Spirit of Love, is our own egoism. We are thinking about ourselves; we are locked into ourselves.

THE THEOLOGY

Saying the mantra is unlocking the door of our heart. The mantra is like the key unlocking the door to allow the pure light of love to flood in. It is a gentle process. Don't expect miracles. In fact, don't expect anything. Be content, humbly, every morning and evening, to return simply to the practice. In the practice itself you will find the gentleness, the compassion and the forgiveness, all revealing themselves.

3.8 Death and Resurrection

Listen to these words of Jesus reported in the Gospel of St John:

In very truth, anyone who gives heed to what I say and puts his trust in him who sent me has hold of eternal life, and does not come up for judgement, but has already passed from death to life. (John 5:24)

Meditation is focused right in the heart, right in the centre of the Christian mystery, and the Christian mystery can only be penetrated if we enter into the mystery of death and resurrection. That is the essential message of Jesus: "No man can be a follower of mine unless he leaves self behind... The man who would find his life must lose it." In the natural examples he gives, the seed must fall into the ground and die, or else it remains alone.

What we do in meditation is refining our perception down to the single point which is Christ. Christ is our way, our goal, our companion. But he is our goal only in the sense that once we are wholly with him, wholly at one with him, we go with him to the Father. In meditation, we come to that single-pointedness which is Christ.

It is impossible to talk about meditation as it is impossible to talk about the Christian experience in any adequate terms. As one philosopher put it, "As soon as we begin to speak of the mysteries of Christ, we hear the gates of heaven closing." Yet we have to try to speak, but we speak only to bring people to silence. It is the silence of our meditation that is our way into the extraordinary mystery to be found within the heart of each one of us, if only we will undertake this pilgrimage to one-pointedness, to single-mindedness. We have to find some way of trying to explain what the journey is, why the journey is so worthwhile, and why it requires courage.

Meditation is a way where we focus our attention, we narrow our attention, down to one point. It seems to me that it might help you to understand what meditation is about if you can see it as a great double triangle.

Here you have the triangle on the top pointing down, and then the triangle underneath it opening out. The triangle on the top is learning to concentrate, learning to focus our attention, entirely upon Christ. In that sense, it is narrowing our attention to that one point. But as soon as we do, the way is opened to infinite expansion on the other side. A single point thus leads us into infinite expansion. It is through Jesus that we pass over from everything that is dead, from everything that is restricted into the infinite expansion of God, which is infinite expansion of love.

As we come to that one-pointedness, we need courage. We need the courage to persevere, not to be afraid of the narrowness, and not to be afraid of the demand that is being made on us. The demand is an absolute demand, the demand of faith, to believe that what Jesus says is true, that if we lose our life, then and only then will we be able to find it.

Meditation is like breaking through the sound barrier. When you come to that point, there can be a lot of turbulence. It is at this moment that the discipline you have learned, by saying your mantra and by faithfully continuing to say it, will enable you to be entirely open to the love of Jesus, which takes you through it. As we approach that point, it seems that we require great courage. It seems that we require great perseverance. What we come to know is that all the courage and all the capacity to persevere are ours, in Jesus.

This is the fantastic basis of the whole Christian mystery – that the Passover is accomplished. It is achieved in Jesus. It is his courage, his faithfulness, and his love, that take us into the infinite expansion that is God. So there is no essential ground for our fear, for our postponement, for our dilatoriness. Everything is ours in the love of Jesus.

The essential axis of Christian life is death and resurrection. The resurrection is to new life, limitless life, eternal life. What Jesus tells us is that if we are open to him, if we have the courage to listen to him, to hear what he says, then eternal life, infinite life, and the infinite expansion of life is ours. That is the mystery. That is what we are invited to be open to. That is what we are invited to proclaim to the world.

4 THE MANTRA

As you persevere with the mantra, you will begin to understand more and more deeply, out of your own experience, what Jesus meant when he said, "Blessed are the poor in spirit."

John Main

4.1	The Grand Poverty of the Mantra
4.2	Choosing Your Mantra
4.3	Stages of Saying the Mantra
4.4	Saying and Sounding the Mantra
4.5	Listening to the Mantra
4.6	Say Your Mantra until You Cannot Say It
4.7	Breathing and the Mantra

4.1 The Grand Poverty of the Mantra

The essential task for the Christian is to understand poverty as the condition of spiritual development, to see prayer as the deepening of our conversion, of our turning from self to God in faith.

The monastic tradition has always emphasized, since Cassian and St Benedict, that poverty is the condition for prayer.

The monastic teaching and tradition of prayer tells us in every generation, all Christians, not just monks, that our prayer is our declaration of poverty, our experience of poverty. And so its teaching on how to pray tells us how to let ourselves be led by the Spirit into a totally generous poverty of spirit. From Cassian until the present day, the monastic tradition has taught what Cassian's Tenth Conference on Prayer calls 'the poverty of the single verse'. We are led to this other-centredness of love, into the prayer of Christ which is the Spirit praying in our hearts, by the simplicity, the humility, the openness, of committing ourselves wholly in our meditation to the recitation of a single word.

John Cassian speaks of the purpose of meditation as that of restricting the mind to the poverty of the single verse. Cassian writes:

> *The mind should unceasingly cling to the* [mantra], *until strengthened by continual use of it, it casts off and rejects the rich and ample matter of all kinds of thought and restricts itself to the poverty of the single verse... Those who realize this poverty arrive with ready ease at the first of the Beatitudes: 'Blessed are they who are poor in spirit, for theirs is the Kingdom of Heaven. [Matt 5:3]'*
> (Conference 10:11)

Cassian talks about becoming 'grandly poor'. Prayer is both the acknowledgement and experience of our own poverty, our own utter dependence on God, who is the source of our being. But it is also the experience of our redemption, our enrichment by the love of God in Jesus. This twin aspect of prayer, of poverty and redemption, leads Cassian to call the condition we enjoy in prayer a 'grand poverty'.

Meditation will certainly give you new insights into poverty. As you persevere with the mantra, you will begin to understand more and more deeply, out of your own experience, what Jesus meant when he said, "Blessed are the poor in spirit." (Matt 5:3) You will also learn in a very concrete way the meaning of faithfulness as you persevere in fidelity to the repetition of the mantra. In meditation, then, we declare our own poverty. We renounce words, thoughts, imaginations, and we do so by restricting the mind to the poverty of the one word. The mantra is the sacrament of our poverty in prayer.

As Cassian puts it, the mantra contains all the human mind can express and all the human heart can feel. That one little word conveys and leads us into the silence which is the silence of creative energy.

Cassian wrote: "The Christian has as his principal aim the realization of the Kingdom of God, the power of the Spirit of Jesus in his heart." But we cannot get this by our own efforts or think our way into it. So we have a simpler, more immediate goal which he calls 'purity of heart'. And this is all we should concern ourselves with, he teaches; the rest will be given to you. And the way to purity of heart, to clear awareness, is the way of poverty, the grand poverty of the mantra.

4.2 Choosing Your Mantra

Choosing your word or mantra is of some importance. Ideally, you should choose your mantra in consultation with your teacher. But there are various mantras which are possible for a beginner. If you have no teacher to help you, then you should choose a word that has been hallowed over the centuries by our Christian tradition. Some of these words were first taken over as mantras for Christian meditation by the Church in its earliest days. One of these is the word *maranatha*. This is the mantra I recommend to most beginners: the Aramaic word *maranatha* which means 'Come Lord. Come Lord Jesus.' It is the word that St Paul uses to end his first letter to the Corinthians (1 Cor 16:22). It is also the word with which St John ends the book of Revelation (Rev 22:20). It also has a place in some of the earliest Christian liturgies (*Didache* 10:6).

I prefer the Aramaic form because it has no associations for most of us, and it helps us into a meditation that will be quite free of all images. The name 'Jesus' would be another possibility as a mantra. So would the word that Jesus himself used in his prayer, namely *Abba*, again an Aramaic word which means 'Father'. The important thing to remember about your mantra is to choose it if possible in consultation with a teacher, and then to keep to it. If you chop and change your mantra, you are postponing your progress in meditation.

When you say your mantra, it's better not to think about the meaning of it. Just say it and listen to it as a sound. The author of *The Cloud of Unknowing* says choose a mantra that is full of meaning, but when you say it, say it whole and entire. Don't think about the meaning. That's very good advice.

The essence of the mantra is that it brings you to silence. It's not a magic word; it's not a word that has any esoteric properties to it, or anything like that. It's simply a word that is sacred in our tradition. Maranatha is possibly the oldest Christian prayer there is after the Our Father. It is a word that brings us to great peacefulness, to rest and calm. Certainly to begin with, I would recommend you to use a word that has at least an open 'a' vowel sound in it. I think the best word you could use to start with is *maranatha*. It is the oldest Christian prayer there is, and it possesses the right sound to bring us to the silence and stillness necessary for meditation.

4.3 Stages of Saying the Mantra

When you start, you will find all sorts of distractions in your mind. The purpose of the mantra is to bring your mind to calm, to peace, to concentration. The only way to do it is to keep saying the mantra.

In starting to meditate, we have three preliminary aims. The first is simply to say the mantra for the full duration of the meditation. It will probably take some time to achieve this first stage, and we will have to learn patience in the mean time.

The second aim is to say the mantra throughout the meditation without interruption, while remaining quite calm in the face of all distractions. In this phase, the mantra resembles a plough that continues resolutely across the rough field of our mind, undeflected by any obtrudance or disturbance.

The third of these preliminary aims is to say the mantra for the entire time of the meditation, quite free of all distractions. The surface areas of the mind are now in tune with the deep peacefulness at the core of our being. The same harmonic sounds throughout our being. In this state, we have passed beyond thought, beyond imagination, and beyond all images. We simply rest with the Reality, the realized presence of God himself dwelling within our hearts.

But we should not waste time and energy worrying about what stage we have reached. "Unless you become like little children, you cannot enter the Kingdom of Heaven." (Matt 18:3) What we must do is to begin to meditate, to begin to open ourselves up to the love of God and its power. To do this, all we need to do is to begin to say the mantra, lovingly and in a deep spirit of faith.

The stages of our progress in meditation will come about in their own time, God's own time. We in fact only hinder this progression by becoming too self-conscious about our stage of development.

THE MANTRA

This is where a teacher is of immense help for keeping you on a straight course. But I must emphasize for you that basically your teacher has only one instruction to give you, and that is to say your mantra. More than this, is simply encouragement and comfort until the mantra is rooted in your consciousness.

4.4 Saying and Sounding the Mantra

Learning to meditate is learning to say the mantra. Because it is as simple as this, we should be quite clear in our understanding of the process of saying the mantra. We must grow in our fidelity to the mantra, and in the same proportion the mantra grows more and more deeply rooted in us.

As you know, the mantra I recommend you to say is the word *maranatha*, the ancient Aramaic prayer which means 'Come Lord. Come Lord Jesus.' I suggest that you articulate it in your mind silently, with equal stress on each of the four syllables: ma-ra-na-tha.

Most of us begin 'saying' the mantra. That is it seems as though we are speaking it with our mind silently somewhere in our head. But, as we make progress, the mantra becomes more familiar, less of a stranger, less of an intruder in our consciousness. We find less effort is required to persevere in saying it throughout the time of our meditation.

Then it seems that we are not so much 'speaking' it in our minds as 'sounding' it in our hearts. This is the stage that we describe as the mantra becoming rooted in our hearts. At this stage of sounding the mantra in our hearts, we might describe it as similar to pushing lightly a pendulum that needs only a slight stimulus to set it swinging in a calm, steady rhythm.

It is at this moment that our meditation is really beginning. We are really beginning to concentrate away from ourselves because, from now on, instead of either saying or sounding the mantra, we begin to listen to it, wrapped in ever-deepening attention. When he described this stage of meditation, my teacher used to say that, from this moment on, it is as though the mantra is sounding in the valley below us while we are toiling up the side of a mountain. Meditation is in essence the art of concentration precisely because the higher we toil up the mountainside the fainter becomes the mantra sounding in the valley below us, and so the more attentively and seriously we have to listen to it.

There then comes the day when we enter that 'cloud of unknowing' in which there is silence, absolute silence, and we can no longer hear the mantra.

When we begin to meditate, we must say the mantra for the whole twenty or thirty minutes of our meditation, whatever mood we are in or whatever reaction we seem to be having. As we progress in fidelity in saying it, we must then sound it for the whole time of our meditation, whatever the distractions or feelings that may arise. Then, as the mantra becomes rooted in our heart, we must listen to it with our whole attention without ceasing.

But we must always remember that we cannot attempt to force the pace of meditation in any way or to speed up the natural process in which the mantra roots itself in our consciousness by means of our simple fidelity in saying it. We must not be self-consciously asking ourselves, "How far have I got? Am I saying the mantra or sounding it or listening to it?" If we try to force the pace or to keep a constant self-conscious eye on our progress, we are, if there is such a word, non-meditating because we are concentrating on ourselves, putting ourselves first, thinking about ourselves.

I repeat this to impress upon you what is the essential and perhaps the only advice worth giving about meditation, which is simply this, I will repeat it again: Say your mantra. This is not an easy doctrine to accept, nor is it easy to follow. We all hope, when we first begin to meditate, for some instant mystical experience, and we tend to over-estimate the first unusual experiences that the process of meditation brings to us. But this is not important. The important thing is to persevere with the mantra, to stabilize ourselves by our discipline which makes us ready for the higher slopes of the mountain.

Meditation requires complete simplicity. We are led to that complete simplicity, but we begin and continue by saying the mantra. So now, begin your meditation in simplicity of heart, and be faithful to your humble task of saying the mantra without ceasing.

4.5 Listening to the Mantra

It is difficult to find a good word to describe the action of actually repeating the mantra. But probably the best word is to 'sound' it silently in your heart. For most people, when they begin to say their mantra, they say it in the head. Then, after you have been saying the mantra for some time, the mantra becomes deeper, more centred in the centre of your being which we describe as the heart. It's in the simple practice of meditation that the mantra just quite naturally sinks deeper into us and begins to sound in the heart. You needn't use any force or any effort to bring that about, but just let it happen when it happens.

Meditating is saying your mantra and listening to it from the beginning to the end, not picturing it at all, but listening to it as a sound. No visualization at all. The imagination must be completely at rest. Just listen to it as a sound. In meditating, you must pass beyond all images. That's why you mustn't imagine the word but you must listen to it as a sound. That's the important thing. Just listen to it.

What you have to do is listen to the mantra. You have to listen to the mantra as the profoundest and most supreme sound in your being. That's learning a very considerable discipline. To learn it, you have to be very patient with yourself, and very faithful to the morning and evening meditation, every day. That's why the constant return to it is so essential.

Effort is not a very good concept to use, because the essence of saying the mantra is really to say it effortlessly but wholeheartedly. What I mean by 'wholeheartedness' is an undivided consciousness. For most of the time, our minds are hopelessly divided. We are thinking about three, four, six, or a dozen things at the same time. We've got all sorts of contrary objectives, incompatible objectives, in our mind. What meditation brings us to is what the Scriptures call an undivided heart.

Our heart is filled with love. Our consciousness is aligned wholly, if you like, on the consciousness of Christ, and so in that sense it is an undivided heart and an undivided consciousness. It's an integration of the whole of your body and the whole of your spirit in the divine consciousness.

The art of meditation is learning to set the mantra free in your heart so that it sounds in your heart at all times as a focal point of stability within the depths of your being. The difficulty of this for us is that we always want to be in control; and it is very difficult for us to learn to set the mantra free, to let is sound and let it sing in our hearts in a sort of glorious liberty.

These words that we use to describe what to do are quite inadequate really to describe the experience. Really the only way of learning it is just to do it yourself. But the thing to do is not to imagine it, not think about it, not think about what it means, or anything like that, but just to say it, to recite it, to listen to it, in the greatest simplicity that you can possibly bring to it.

4.6 Say Your Mantra until You Cannot Say It

Let me stress for you again the importance of the daily fidelity to meditation, every morning and every evening, and of the fidelity to your word.

We had a group of priests here this morning from the Montreal area, and one of them, who is beginning meditation, made the point: "Surely if you have a holy thought, a religious thought while you are meditating, surely you should follow it." I think the thing to understand is this: In saying the mantra with growing and indeed perfect fidelity, we are not attending to any thought about God. We are attending to his real presence in our own hearts and in all creation. In attending to that presence, any thought is a distraction. Our invitation is to become wholly absorbed in him, to be one with him.

There is no point where you give up saying your mantra. There is a point when you cease to say it. I don't recommend you to think too much about that when you are beginning, but basically speaking, the process is like this. But one again must never be self-conscious about it. One must never be trying to make it happen. You say your mantra every morning and every evening, for about twenty years or so. Then, one morning or one evening, you are aware that you are not saying your mantra. As soon as you are aware that you are not saying it, you start saying it again. Those times of 'not saying' the mantra might be a split second, might be three minutes, might be the whole half an hour. But if you are aware that for the whole half-an-hour you have not been saying your mantra, you can be sure that you are not meditating, whatever else you were doing! A really important principle to get clear in your mind is: "Say your mantra until you cannot say it." As soon as you are aware that you are not saying it, say it again. The way that the ancient monastic tradition expressed that was, "The monk who knows he is praying is not praying; the monk who does not know he is praying is praying."

Say the word as selflessly as you can: ma-ra-na-tha. And continue to say it. Continue to say your word for the whole time of the meditation. Return to it if you had let it go. Don't bother about distractions; just keep saying your word. As you do so, you enter into, descend into, areas of simplicity in yourself you hardly suspected were there, areas of humility in yourself that you had forgotten were there, your capacity to be childlike, to be trusting, and to leave all demands and all desire behind.

4.7 Breathing and the Mantra

Breathing while you are meditating is like the breathing at all other times. You breathe in order to keep going; you are not very conscious about it.

The best way to say the mantra is to breathe in the mantra and breathe out in silence. Sometimes, people find that a four-syllable mantra like *maranatha* is too much for their lungs and they can't breathe it all in. If you can't, while you are learning to breathe more deeply, then you can breathe in *mara*, and breathe out *natha*. But, probably, the best way to say the mantra is to breathe it all in, and to breathe out in silence. Some people, on the other hand, can't say the mantra to their breathing at all, and say the mantra to their heartbeat. Others can't hear their heartbeat. So it's a very personal thing. If there is a 'best' way of saying it, the best way is to breathe it in and to breathe out in silence.

When you begin however to say your mantra breathing it in, you become a bit more conscious about that breathing, as you do of yourself sitting still meditating and saying your mantra – you have got to try and remember the whole thing. The very purpose of saying the mantra on a daily basis morning and evening is that you build it into your natural systems so that it does become eventually a wholly unself-conscious process. You 'forget' that you are meditating, in that sense. The important thing is to try (a phrase I sometimes use) to root the mantra in your heart. Once it is rooted there, you breathe it in and you breathe out in silence utterly unself-consciously. Ma-ra-na-tha. If you can do it, breathe it in in one breath and breathe it out silently. Saying the mantra is like your acceptance of God's Spirit, which is your life, which you breathe in and so live. Breathing out in silence is, as it were, returning your life to him with absolute faith and with absolute love, ready to receive it from him again should he give it back to you.

I don't like to say too much about breathing at the beginning because in the West we tend to be obsessed by techniques. We have to discover that meditating is the most natural thing in the world; it's what we were created to do – to be in absolute harmony with the Creator. So the least complication you bring to it when you are beginning, the better.

5 THE TRADITION

The mantra has been in the Christian tradition of prayer from the beginning, the understanding that prayer is beyond the operations of the mind.

John Main

5.1	What the Tradition Tells Us
5.2	The Tradition of the Mantra
5.3	Purity of Heart
5.4	John Cassian
5.5	The Mantra in Christian Prayer

5.1 What the Tradition Tells Us

We speak to you as Benedictine monks. Our message to you is that we are the inheritors, you and I, in this time, of a long and rich spiritual tradition. It's a tradition that has been passed on and has survived for hundreds of years despite many attacks on it, despite many misunderstandings of it, and despite simple neglect.

The tradition that we speak out of is the tradition of the prayer of John Cassian in the Desert and the Benedictine tradition, particularly as enshrined in *The Cloud of Unknowing* written in the fourteenth century in England, in the writings of Abbot Chapman in the twentieth century in England. All that tradition over the centuries says to us that the supreme task for every life that would be fully alive, fully human, is to be as open as we can be to that life of Jesus within us.

Consider for a moment what the tradition tells us. The tradition tells us that Jesus lives in our hearts. We have all read that in the scriptures. We all know it at one level. Listen to St Paul here:

> *Continually, while still alive, we are being surrendered into the hands of death, for Jesus' sake, so that the life of Jesus also may be revealed in this mortal body of ours.* (2 Cor 4:11)

That is the conviction of the early Church, that the life of Jesus is being progressively and more profoundly revealed within each one of us. That we have to keep absolutely clear, because Christianity isn't in essence a theory or a theology; it is in essence openness to the person of Jesus Christ. In that openness, we are taken by him to the Father. Christianity is the religion of transcendence – transcending our own limited life and entering into the limitless life of God.

Now that being the essential theology, what is our response to that? What does the tradition tell us about the way? The tradition tells us that we must learn to be disciplined. We must learn to leave self behind, which is another way of saying that we must learn to leave the limitations of self behind and we must be open to the being of God. Make no mistake about it. Christianity proclaims an astonishing doctrine. St Paul writes:

> *Indeed, it is for your sake that all things are ordered, so that, as the abounding grace of God is shared by more and more, the greater may be the chorus of thanksgiving that ascends to the glory of God.* (2 Cor 4:15)

This is the doctrine that we have to be open to. This is the person that we have to be open to. The tradition tells us that we must learn discipline, and we must learn simplicity. Hence the need for our daily meditation, every morning and every evening, and during the time of our meditation to learn to be profoundly silent. That we do by reciting our word.

The author of *The Cloud of Unknowing* says confine the whole activity of your being to the recital of one little word. The recitation of the word will teach you many things. It will teach you humility. It will teach you poverty, that you surrender all the richness of words, all your ideas, to be open to the supreme reality, the infinity of God that cannot be captured in any concept, in any idea, in any intellectual formula, but that can be encountered in your own heart, in the depth of your being, where you are open to the being of God.

Meditating is not thinking about God, not thinking about theology or thinking about religion. Meditating is something much greater than that. It's *being* with God. When you begin you have to take that on faith. You take it on the faith of godly men and women throughout the ages who have confronted the basic theology that

Jesus lives, and that he lives in our hearts. They have confronted it and sought to make the truth of it the main thrust of their lives. That's their tradition.

When we sit down to meditate, we put ourselves in touch with a great and glorious tradition of men and women who throughout the ages have understood that the greatest wisdom is to leave self behind; men and women who have understood the words of Jesus "unless you leave yourself behind, you cannot be my disciple"; men and women who have set out on this path whereby we leave behind all our own limitations and enter into the infinite generosity of God's love.

5.2 The Tradition of the Mantra

To many ordinary churchgoers and many priests, monks and sisters, the mantra seems at first a suspiciously new-fangled technique of prayer, or like some exotic trick-method, or some kind of therapy that may help you to relax, but has no claim to be called Christian. This is a desperately sad state of affairs. So many Christians have lost touch with their own tradition of prayer. We no longer benefit as we should from the wisdom and experienced counsel of the great masters of prayer.

All these masters have agreed that in prayer it is not we ourselves who are taking the initiative. We are not talking to God. We are listening to his Word within us. We are not looking for him; it is *he* who has found us.

Walter Hilton expressed it very simply in the fourteenth century. He wrote, "You, yourself, do nothing; you simply allow him to work in your soul." The advice of St Theresa was in tune with this. She reminds us that all we can do in prayer is to dispose ourselves; the rest is in the power of the Spirit who leads us. What Hilton and St Theresa are showing us is the same experience of prayer as that which led St Paul to write that "we do not even know how to pray, but the Spirit prays within us" (Rom 8:26). What this means in the language of our own day is that before we can pray, we have first to become still, to concentrate. Only then can we enter into a loving awareness of the Spirit of Jesus within our heart.

St Teresa of Avila was of the opinion that if you were serious about prayer you would be led into what she called 'the prayer of quiet' within a relatively short time, six months or a year. St John of the Cross said the principal sign of your readiness for silence in prayer was that your discursive thinking at the time of prayer was becoming evidently a distraction and counter-productive.

The mantra is an ancient tradition. We find it in the ancient Jewish custom of 'blessing the Lord at all times'. We find the mantra in the early Christian Church. We may find it, for example, in the Our Father which was a series of short rhythmic phrases in the original Aramaic. We find it too in the Orthodox tradition of the Jesus Prayer, the prayer that Jesus himself commended: "Lord, be merciful to me, a sinner." (Luke 18:13)

The prayer of Jesus himself as recorded in the Gospel leads to the same conclusions. "Lord, teach us to pray," his disciples asked him. His teaching was simplicity itself:

> *When you pray, do not be like the hypocrites... but go into a room by yourself, shut the door and pray to your Father who is there in the secret place...Do not go babbling on like the heathens who imagine that the more they say, the more likely they are to be heard. Your Father knows what your needs are before you ask him. (Matt 6:5-8)*

In the Garden of Gethsemane, Jesus is described as praying over and over again "in the same words" (Mark 14:39, Matt 26:44). Whenever he addresses the Father for the sake of the crowd, the word Abba is always on his lips, the same word which St Paul describes the Spirit of Jesus eternally crying in our hearts.

Time and again, the practical advice of masters of prayer is summed up in the simple injunction: "Say your mantra". "Use this little word," *The Cloud of Unknowing* advises, "and pray not in many words but in a little word of one syllable. Fix this word fast to your heart so that it is always there come what may. With this word, you will suppress all thoughts." (ch 7, 39)

Abbot Chapman, in his famous letter of Michaelmas 1920 from Downside, describes the simple, faithful use of a mantra which he had discovered more from his own courageous perseverance in prayer than from teachers. He had rediscovered a simple enduring tradition of prayer that entered the West through monasticism, and first entered Western monasticism through John Cassian in the late fourth century. Cassian himself received it from the holy men of the desert who placed its origin back beyond living memory, back to Apostolic times.

The venerable tradition of the mantra in Christian prayer is above all attributable to its utter simplicity. It answers all the requirements of the masters' advice on how to pray because it leads us to a harmonious attentive stillness of mind, body and spirit. It requires no special talent or gift apart from serious intent and the courage to persevere. "No one," Cassian said, "is kept away from purity of heart by not being able to read, nor is rustic simplicity any obstacle to it, for it lies close at hand for all if only they will by constant repetition of this phrase keep the mind and heart attentive to God."

Our mantra is the ancient Aramaic prayer: "Maranatha. Maranatha. Come Lord. Come Lord Jesus."

5.3 Purity of Heart

The early Fathers of the Church describe the call to meditation as a call to purity of heart, a vision unclouded by egoism or by desire or by images, a heart simply moved by love.

Purity of heart is a wonderful concept that appears very early in the tradition. The early Fathers of the monastic movement saw that purity of heart was *the* necessary condition for the whole purpose of the Christian life, which they saw as being to see God with absolute clarity. Meditation is our way to that clarity of vision. The skill we have to learn is to see what is there: "Blessed are the pure of heart, for they shall see God."

Meditation leads us to this clarity – clarity of vision, clarity of understanding, and clarity of love – a clarity that comes from simplicity.

The school or teaching that we follow is that of John Cassian who represented the teaching of the earliest monastic Fathers. He was teaching a tradition that depended upon the human quality of fidelity, and daily practice was the essence of that fidelity.

We have to be very careful when we are looking at meditation not to be taken in by mere techniques. The essence of meditation is not the technique but what John Cassian called 'purity of heart'. What he says in his writings is that the essence of meditation, the end of meditation, the purpose of meditation, is the Kingdom of God, that is God's power released, having its full sway in our hearts. What he goes on to say is that before we can move to this ultimate aim we have to undergo a preliminary step. The preliminary step he calls 'purity of heart'. That is the aim of all meditation – to purify our heart.

Now we must beware of thinking that we can do this merely by techniques. The method is important, but it is our *approach* to it that is more important. We approach it in a simple, human fashion. This is the important thing to understand, that purity of heart is the first step that we take. We are used to finding techniques that produce instant results. The tradition that we speak from is not a tradition that is technique-oriented nor instant-oriented. The tradition that we speak from, and that John Cassian was a great exemplar of, is one of infinite gentleness, infinite patience and total fidelity.

Purity of heart is learning to see clearly. So often our vision is clouded by our own egoism, our own desire. So often we see others in terms of their usefulness to us or their service to us: "What will they do for me?" Insofar as we do, we do not see them clearly, we do not see them as they are. If we do not see them as they are, we cannot love them. Again, that is the whole purpose of our Christian commitment. The final end: the Kingdom of God, the vision of God. The Kingdom of God is simply that state where all of us live out of God's power, live out of his power of love, live within the ambiance of his love, communicate and expand his love in our hearts, in our lives, in our relationships.

The first step is purity of heart. That means doing what the author of *The Cloud of Unknowing* calls 'loosening the root of sin within us'. Another way of putting that is learning to be free, learning to live out of the infinite liberty of God and not to be constrained by our own possessiveness, our own desire, our own selfishness. That is the high road to liberty and to joy – not to try to dominate one another, to impress one another, but to love one another. That is what the joy of the Christian vision of reality is.

The method that we have from John Cassian, from *The Cloud of Unknowing* a thousand years later, is very simple: to meditate every day, every morning and every evening. The time: a minimum when you start of about twenty minutes, and the optimum time about half an hour. During the meditation you have to learn to do one thing: to say your mantra. The mantra is a word, and you simply learn to recite that word from the beginning to the end. It is difficult to see when you start that it is the word itself that is so important, that that is the way to freedom. You recite the word paying attention to it and leaving behind your own thoughts, your own desires, your own feelings, your own imagination.

The essence of meditation is to stop thinking about yourself and to listen to the word. The difficulty of it is that it reduces you down to a point of zero, and you want to think about yourself. You want to ask, "Am I making progress? Am I getting nearer to enlightenment? Is this actually working?" But you must abandon all those thoughts, and you have to take it on faith that it is being reduced to that zero point that takes you through on the other side, into the infinity of God's love. We must learn to empty our heart of everything that is not God, for he requires all the room that our heart can offer. We learn that purity of heart by saying our mantra with absolute fidelity. The mystery is absolute truth, absolute love, and our response too must be absolute. But you have to take it on faith that it is the daily return, every morning and every evening to the recitation of that word in absolute faith and fidelity, that will gradually bring you to that point of pure nothingness. It is at that point of pure nothingness that you enter into the mystery of God.

5.4 John Cassian

Throughout Christian history, men and women of prayer have fulfilled a special mission in bringing their contemporaries, and even succeeding generations, to enlightenment, the rebirth in spirit that Jesus preached.

One of these teachers, John Cassian, in the fourth century, has a claim to be one of the most influential teachers of the spiritual life in the West, as the teacher and inspirer of St Benedict and so of the whole of Western monasticism.

Cassian's own pilgrimage began with his own search for a teacher, for a master of prayer, a master he could not find in his own monastery in Bethlehem. Just as thousands of young people today make their pilgrimage to the East in search of wisdom and personal authority, so Cassian and his friend Germanus journeyed to the deserts of Egypt where the holiest and most famous men of the Spirit were to be found in the fourth century.

It was in listening with total attention to the teachings of the Holy Abbot Isaac that Cassian was first fired with an enthusiasm for prayer and the firm resolve to persevere. Abbot Isaac spoke eloquently and sincerely but, as Cassian concludes his first Conference:

> *With these words of the Holy Isaac, we were dazzled rather than satisfied ... since we felt that though the excellence of prayer had been shown to us, still we had not yet understood its nature and the power by which continuance in it might be gained and kept.* (Conference 9:36)

His experience was clearly similar to that of many today who have heard inspiring accounts of prayer but are left uninstructed as to the practical means of really becoming aware of the Spirit praying in their hearts.

Cassian and Germanus humbly returned to Abbot Isaac after a few days with the simple question: "How do we pray? Teach us, show us." His answer to their question: Prayer is both the acknowledgement and experience of our own poverty, our own utter dependence on God who is the source of our being. But it is also the experience of our redemption, our enrichment by the love of God in Jesus. These twin aspects of prayer, of poverty and redemption, lead Cassian to call the condition we enjoy in prayer a 'grand poverty'.

The simple practical means he teaches is the unceasing use of the mantra.

> *The mind should unceasingly cling to the [mantra], until strengthened by continual use of it, it casts off and rejects the rich and ample matter of all kinds of thought and restricts itself to the poverty of the single verse... Those who realize this poverty arrive with ready ease at the first of the Beatitudes: 'Blessed are they who are poor in spirit, for theirs is the Kingdom of Heaven. [Matt 5:3]'* (Conference 10:11)

The spiritual life for Cassian, the serious perseverance in the poverty of the single verse, is a passover. By persevering, we pass from sorrow to joy, from loneliness to communion, the unbroken awareness of the life of the Spirit continually renewing us, giving new life to our mortal bodies.

"The Christian," he wrote, "has as his principal aim the realization of the Kingdom of God, the power of the Spirit of Jesus in his heart." But we cannot get this by our own efforts or think our way into it, and so we have a simpler and more immediate goal which he calls 'purity of heart'. "This is all we should concern ourselves with," he teaches, "the rest will be given to us."

And the way to purity of heart, to full and clear awareness, is the way of poverty, the 'grand poverty' of the mantra.

5.5 The Mantra in Christian Prayer

The mantra has been in the Christian tradition of prayer from the beginning. The understanding that prayer is beyond the operations of the mind is to be found in every authoritative statement.

St Ignatius of Loyola, in the *Spiritual Exercises*, wrote: "If this passover is to be perfect, we must set aside all discursive operations of the intellect and turn the very apex of our soul to God, to be entirely transformed in him."

The mantra spans levels of consciousness and dimensions of time. It is, in a sense, our echoing response to the love-cry of the Spirit, to the whole life of Jesus returning to the Father. A response not at any level of conceptual reasoning, but an absolute, unconditional response, insofar as we are aware of it, at the deepest level of our being where we acknowledge and experience our complete poverty and complete dependence upon the sustaining love of God. Our response achieves this absolute value, travels to this source level of our being, to the extent that we say the mantra with complete simplicity and persevere in our renunciation, at the time of our meditation, of our thoughts, imaginations, of our very self-consciousness. As the mantra becomes more deeply rooted and thoroughly integrated with our consciousness, so does our whole being participate in our response to the Spirit. Its purpose is that integration of all our levels of being with the source of our being, the source that calls the whole person back into itself, awakened through the Spirit of Jesus. Our aim is the realization of our whole being.

There is no doubt of the absolute demand of the mantra. In essence it is our acceptance of the absoluteness of God's love flooding our heart through the Spirit of the risen Jesus. Our death consists in the relentless simplicity of the mantra and the absolute renunciation of thought and language at the time of our meditation.

The mantra creates the possibility of such an integration. It prepares us as a living sacrifice to the Lord. It leads us in all simplicity to the seminal Christian experience, the prayer of the Spirit in our heart.

The fruits of that experience are the fruits of the Spirit. Perhaps the first discovery we make that opens the way to all these gifts of the Spirit is that of our own personal and infinite loveableness. We cannot manufacture or anticipate the experience; we can only learn to be still, to be silent, and to wait with an ever-growing sense of our own harmony. The fruits of the Spirit are given with and grow out of the experience of the Spirit of Jesus, flooding our hearts with God's personal love and summoning us to the fullness of our personhood in our personal encounter with Jesus: "By their fruits you shall know them." (Matt 7:16)

The renewal and enrichment of the Church, and its reinstatement as an authoritative voice in men's lives, depends upon its members' receiving this experience in the depths of their own hearts. Each member of the Church is called to this awakening as a present reality. Each will receive it in the way suited to his own unique personhood, within the plan for his fulfilment held in the mysterious love of God.

I am not saying that meditation is the only way. I am simply saying that it is the only way I have found. In my own experience it is the way of pure simplicity that enables us to become fully, integrally, aware of the Spirit Jesus has sent into our heart. This is the recorded experience of the mainstream of the Christian tradition from Apostolic times down to our own day.

6 THE JOURNEY

Meditation is ... the art of all arts... Once you understand that meditation is an art, you begin to understand that the practice of it is much more important than all the speculation about it.

John Main

6.1   Set Your Mind on the Kingdom
6.2   Self-Transcendence
6.3   To Persevere
6.4   Meditation as an Art
6.5   Without Expectations
6.6   Psychical Phenomena
6.7   Progress in the Stillness
6.8   Not My Way, but The Way
6.9   The Ultimate Aim of Meditation

6.1 Set Your Mind on the Kingdom

Listen to these words from the Gospel of Matthew:

The Kingdom of Heaven is like treasure lying buried in a field. The man who found it, buried it again; and for sheer joy went and sold everything he had, and bought that field.
    Here is another picture of the Kingdom of Heaven. A merchant, looking out for fine pearls, found one of very special value; so he went and sold everything he had, and bought it. (Matt 13:44-46)

That's the sort of commitment that we need – the commitment to meditate every day and, in our meditation, to say the mantra from the beginning to the end. A daily commitment, and a commitment that goes totally beyond what we feel. We do not meditate when we feel like it, or not meditate when we do not feel like it. We accept the discipline of the daily meditation, and the daily return to it.

All of us I think, when we are beginning, come to this point where we ask ourselves, "What am I getting out of this? What is it doing for me? Or is this like everything else? Am I going to end up here too with nothing but sterility?" The temptation, of course, is to give up. That's why meditation is such a strange process. It takes time for our conscious mind to keep abreast with what is happening in our deepest being. We are slow to understand the transformation that is taking place. That is why it is so important simply to continue, day after day, morning and evening, and to continue saying the mantra.

What you will know from your own experience is that there are no half-measures. We cannot be half-committed. Just as in meditation itself, its absolute simplicity is that we either say our mantra or we do not. We cannot half say it. And so I want to urge you tonight to commit yourselves, or perhaps better, to allow yourselves to be committed, to say your mantra.

You may ask, "How long will this take?" The answer is it takes only as long as it takes you to desire *one* thing – to set your mind on the Kingdom. In that setting of your mind on the Kingdom, Jesus tells us, everything else is given to you. Every desire is fulfilled. It doesn't matter how long it takes. The only thing that matters is that each of us, according to our own capacity, is on the way. That means finding the time, probably involving a great deal of sacrifice, to meditate every morning and every evening. The minimum time is about twenty minutes; the optimum time is thirty minutes. And what will you be doing at that time? Setting your mind on the Kingdom. Nothing else.

6.2 Self-Transcendence

The essence of the Gospel message, and the essence of the experience of meditation, is not self-analysis but self-transcendence. As Jesus puts it, "If anyone would be a follower of mine, he must leave self behind." (Matt 16:24)

A great deal of the interest in the spiritual life in our time has a psychological origin. People are often interested in what prayer, in what meditation, can teach them about themselves. It's very easy for people of our generation to see everything in terms of self-improvement, self-understanding, and so forth. In fact, of course, this fascination that we have for looking at ourselves can be disastrous for the spiritual journey. There is a real danger that, if we take up meditation and do begin to see that we are understanding ourselves better and then begin to follow this line of discovery, we quickly find that we have left the pilgrimage of meditation, which is a pilgrimage into unlimited knowledge and wisdom. We find that we end up stuck in the limited knowledge of isolation, our own isolation. There is a very real danger that we become as it were entranced by ourselves, by our own mental operations, so entranced that we forget that we are on a pilgrimage into the mystery of God. As Jesus puts it, "If anyone would be a follower of mine, he must leave self behind." (Matt 16:24)

There is no doubt that there is something arduous and demanding about the journey. It requires nerve to take the attention off yourself, to let go of your ideas, and to gaze wholeheartedly ahead. The person meditating is like the eye that can see but cannot see itself. So this is a journey that requires faith, that is commitment. The commitment is to what is beyond yourself, what is greater than yourself. So the journey requires humility, the humility to stop thinking about yourself. What this means is that, as we advance on the journey, we must continually let go of what we think we have achieved. The problem is, when we start, we are always concerned with our progress, with how perfectly we are fulfilling the techniques, and so forth. We must learn that we have to let go. This is the challenge, and it's the challenge that in practical terms requires us to keep saying the mantra from the beginning of our meditation until the end. That's something that you must understand absolutely clearly. If you want to learn to meditate, it is necessary to meditate every day, every morning and every evening and it's necessary, while you are meditating, to say the mantra from the beginning until the end. Whatever thoughts come into your mind, whether they are good thoughts, religious thoughts, holy thoughts, or bad thoughts, let them go and say the mantra. That means that we avoid all the business of rating ourselves in terms of success or failure, in terms of progression or regression. Meditating is the way of learning just to *be*. To be who you are in the presence of God; to be who you are in complete simplicity. And that's what the mantra leads us to when we learn to be faithful to it.

6.3 To Persevere

The important thing in meditating is to persevere – to meditate every morning and every evening, and to persevere saying the mantra from the beginning until the end of the meditation. That takes some doing. Do not be impatient with yourself. You are always bound to say when you begin: "This is a complete waste of time. That guy has to be crazy. I can't sit here just saying this word for a whole half-hour." No one, I think, who has ever meditated, has not had the same experience in meditating. We begin to say our mantra, and then our mind wanders off. Now the important thing to understand is this: When you are meditating, say your mantra as faithfully as you can. If you find your mind has wandered off, start again and keep coming back to it. You will also find that probably you will give up meditating; you will try it for three weeks, maybe for three months. The important thing is to come back to it. The essential is that you meditate every morning and every evening.

Don't be discouraged by failure. We all fail. No one, I think, who has ever meditated, has not begun, stopped; begun again, stopped; given up, started again. If you give up meditating for a day or a week or a month or a year, come back to it, start again.

Everything depends on the practice. It's not good enough to read books about meditation. The fewer books you read about it, the better. It's not just good enough to admire it from a distance. What is essential is that each of us, wherever we are on the pilgrimage, whether we have been meditating for a week, a decade or however long, what is important is that every day, we start, we go back to the beginning, and we tread the pilgrimage humbly, faithfully, and lovingly.

6.4 Meditation as an Art

Meditation has always been understood, in the tradition, as an art. It is an art. And this is a helpful way of looking at it, because it reminds us that it is a process of learning to be at one with our art. If you have ever seen a great violinist playing, the violinist and the violin become one in the exercise of the art. As we look at it, it seems absolutely effortless. Whenever I have heard Isaac Stern or Yehudi Menuhin playing, in watching them I have been quite certain that I could do it just as well. It looks so easy. But of course the facility that the great artists have at being at one with their art comes from their practice, their daily practice. An artist of the eminence of Yehudi Menuhin even now practises for four hours every day.

Learning to meditate is a gradual process, and the most important element in it is the practice. We must meditate every day. We cannot approach meditating hoping that we are going to be experts, proficient within a week or two, or within a year or two. What we require is the regular practice of meditating every morning and evening and the constant commitment to the practice. You can read all the books in the world about playing the flute, but until you pick up a flute and start to play, you will not really have begun. Once you understand that meditation is an art, you begin to understand that the practice of it is much more important than all the rational speculation about it. And so we must understand that to learn to meditate we need discipline – the discipline of sitting down and sitting still and of saying our word, our mantra, from the beginning of our meditation until the end. This is a difficult thing to understand when you begin.

As we start to meditate, we discover that we are full of distractions. I think you have to be patient with the distractions that come. One of the humbling things about learning to meditate is that you can't just switch off the sound track. You think you can.

If anyone had asked you before, you would say, "I am completely in control of my thoughts. If I don't want to think about that, I won't." But when you start to meditate, you discover that, for most people, there isn't just one sound track, but maybe a dozen all competing in a kind of Tower of Babel. You will find, by constantly ignoring the sound tracks, that they give up, the sound track just runs out. That is the reason why – because you ignore it. Learning to ignore it is the great discipline of meditation. The really important thing is just to be committed to saying the mantra as best you can. That's the whole art of meditation.

The advice that I would give you is: try to the very best of your ability just to keep saying the mantra. It seems much more difficult than it is. It is like swimming or like riding a bicycle. If you see a bicycle for the first time as a child, you look at it and you think it is impossible – no one could possibly stay on those two wheels and keep going, you are bound to fall off. And you get on the thing and tense every muscle in your body, and you do fall off. So you say, "There you are, what did I tell you? It's impossible." It is the same with meditating. We do approach it from a very tense starting-point. But if you can only stay there, the gentleness and the compassion and the peace and the love of God will overwhelm you.

You need not be at all concerned about your distractions. They are only a cause for humility. It is an extraordinary thing – here we are, living in the most sophisticated culture that has been known on the face of the earth, with all the advantages we have of education and reading, and all the skills we have, and we cannot sit still for ten seconds! So it should make us humble. Just persevere with that and say your mantra.

You have to be gentle when you start. But what I would say is, if you do find that you have to give up, say in the first week of meditating, well, maybe you had better give up. But in the second week, out of the seven days only give up on six, not on all seven, and gradually try and extend it.

6.5 Without Expectations

When we begin, we are likely to come to meditation with all sorts of expectations – that it is going to bring us peace, it's going to help us concentrate better, it's going to help us in our personal relationships, or whatever.

One of the principal things we have to learn in meditation is to meditate without expectations. We have to learn that the road we are treading is the path of dispossession. We must learn to let go of our desire for wisdom, for knowledge, for holiness, or whatever. Once we begin to enter into the experience of prayer in our meditation, we begin to understand the limiting factors that would be involved in praying for things, for limited things; in desiring things, limited things. We begin to appreciate the sheer wonder of the experience of prayer itself, the wonder of entering into the limitlessness of Christ's prayer, of entering the uncharted seas of the divine reality, to describe which there are no words available. We begin to learn in the experience of our meditation that praying for things is so often indulging our own desires. We must be very clear about this. We must pass beyond all desire.

We are not meditating in order to get some sort of insight. In fact, we are not meditating to gain any possession whatsoever. Quite the reverse. We are meditating so that we can dispossess ourselves, not just of our ideas and insights, but to dispossess ourselves of our very selves. The essence of Christian meditation is that we become absorbed in God, where we lose all sense of ourselves and find ourselves only in God. As the great mystic St Catherine of Genoa wrote: "I know myself only in God." Now that's a very difficult concept for us to come to terms with, because we are all brought up to be such materialists. We are all brought up to be such possessors, such controllers. To sit down and to voluntarily make ourselves poor, dispossess ourselves, as we enter into the presence of God, is a real challenge for us. I think it is the experience of a large number of meditators, particularly the beginners, that it will often seem that the half-hour you spend in meditating in the morning and in the evening seems to be a complete and utter waste of time. You will get up from your meditation and you will say, "Now what did I get out of that?" Nothing. "What happened?" Nothing. Basically speaking, it doesn't matter what happens. All that matters is that you say your mantra and you continue to say it for the entire time of the meditation.

6.6 Psychical Phenomena

When you are beginning to meditate, often all sorts of psychical phenomena can be present. For some people, those who might like to think of themselves as more normal, nothing at all happens. Other people, maybe those who have more imagination, will experience sometimes seeing colours or cloud formations or hearing beautiful singing. But the important thing is to go straight through all these phenomena. They are not at all important in themselves. They are much more likely to be associated with your liver and what you had for supper than with any deep spiritual significance. The important thing is to say the mantra in a growing spirit of poverty and fidelity. That's the really important thing.

One of the most difficult things for Westerners to understand is that meditation is not about trying to make something happen. All of us are so tied in to techniques and production that we almost have to think that in meditation, we are trying to make something happen. What that something is depends a bit on our imagination, whether we are trying to see visions or see flashes of blinding light or whatever it is. The first thing to understand is that meditation is nothing whatever to do with making something happen.

It sometimes happens that as you are meditating, particularly when you are beginning, a great feeling of peacefulness overtakes you. Then you say to yourself, "This is rather marvellous. Where is this going to lead me? What is this about? Let me experience this." And you stop saying your mantra. The likelihood is that as soon as you do, the sense of peace is lost. But there is usually worse to follow because, having lost the sense of peace, you are determined to try and recapture it again. So you start saying your mantra more loudly or wildly to try to possess once more that feeling of peace. But meditation, as St John of the Cross described it, is the way of *dis*-possession.

We are not trying to possess God, or to get him to give us graces, consolation, or a high of some kind, or anything. We are meditating because it is necessary that we should meditate. So we meditate without demands, without any sort of materialistic objective.

Meditation is about deep conversion of heart. This is what we are turning to as we learn to be still, learn to be aware that God has revealed himself to humanity in Jesus and that Jesus reveals himself to us, in our hearts, by his Spirit which he has sent to dwell in our hearts. We must be as fully open as we can be in this life to this Spirit.

Now let me remind you again of the way. It's a way of simplicity. It's a way that requires childlike trust and childlike wonder. Not looking for anything to happen, for any insights or wisdom or any sort of exterior phenomena. All these are trivia compared to the reality that is. The reality that *is*, we know from our Christian faith, is that the Spirit of God dwells in the heart of each one of us. We must turn aside from everything that is passing, from everything that is temporary, and instead open our hearts to what is enduring: to God and to his love for you and for me.

6.7 Progress in the Stillness

People often ask me, "What sort of progress can I expect to make in my meditation?" I think it is important for us to understand at the beginning that our progress is not to be found in anything else but stillness.

If you ask yourself what sort of progress am I making, don't ask yourself "Am I levitating?" or "Am I seeing visions?" That has nothing to do with it. Indeed, if you are seeing visions or levitating, it is more likely due to your diet, drinking too much soda-water, than to the Spirit! So don't be concerned, as it were, with the phenomena of meditation. This is a big problem for so many of our contemporaries – and we are all affected by it – that we are concerned with the phenomena.

The progress is in the stillness. That's what you have to try to understand. It's difficult for us to understand, as people living in the sort of society we live in, because we should be, as it were, achieving goals. There's the first stage and the second stage. Someone sent me the other day a programme of some school of spirituality, and it made hilarious reading. There were courses for beginners in spirituality; there were then courses in advanced spirituality and super-advanced spirituality, all of which could be attended provided you had the requisite credits in the earlier courses. Now, that has very little to do with the reality of what St Paul is writing about. Just listen to these words of St Paul writing to the Ephesians:

> *So he came and proclaimed the good news: peace to you who are far off, and peace to those who are near by; for through him we both alike have access to the Father in the one Spirit.* (Eph 2:17)

Those are magnificent words of St Paul. The message we have to hear from them is that Jesus has achieved all this. He has, as it were, opened the highway to the Father for us. We don't have to do anything ourselves to bring that about. That's the way it is. We have access to the Father in him, and all we have to do is to realize this. That's what meditation is about. It's about opening our heart, opening our consciousness to the great reality that is taking place in our heart. In our heart, the Spirit of Jesus worships the Father, loves the Father, returns to him in love.

Do not think of your meditation as the icing on the cake of your day. It is not 'putting a bit of spirituality' into your day. See it as informing your whole day with reality, the supreme reality that we have access to God. Meditation is simply openness to that reality. So when you think of progress, think only of progress in stillness, in silence. In your physical posture, be as still as you can. As your heart fills with wonder at the unfathomable mystery that we are part of, be more deeply still. Progress is only progress in fidelity.

Don't be looking for results. The only thing to look for is your own fidelity in being at your meditation in the morning and being at your meditation in the evening, and during your meditation, saying your word from beginning to end. That's the only way that you will learn to meditate. As I say, forget results to begin with, at least for the first twenty years or so. After that, you won't be bothered about results anyway. The essence of it is the daily fidelity, and the fidelity during the meditation to saying the mantra from beginning to end.

6.8 Not My Way but The Way

People ask, "How long will this take? I have been meditating every morning and every evening for six months, and I am not sure if it has made any difference yet." The answer to that is that it doesn't matter how long it takes. All that matters is that we are on the way, on the pilgrimage, and that daily – perhaps only by one centimetre at a time – but daily our commitment to truth and to freedom grows. The growth is often imperceptible, but that does not matter. All that matters is that we are growing, that we have not settled for half, and that we have not betrayed the gift of our own being, but we are committed to growth and to maturity.

The stages of our progress in meditation will come about in their own time. God's own time. We in fact only hinder this progression by becoming too self-conscious about our stage of development. There are, of course, stages we pass through en route to the full realization of the Kingdom of God within us. But we should not waste time and energy worrying about what stage we have reached. "Unless you become like little children, you cannot enter the Kingdom of Heaven." (Matt 18:3) What we must do is to begin to meditate, to begin to open ourselves up to the love of God and its power. To do this, all we need to do is to begin to say the mantra, lovingly and in a deep spirit of faith.

The great thing we have to understand is this, that the summons we have from Jesus is to follow the Way, not my way, but *the* Way. That is very difficult for us as modern men and women to understand because almost everything in our experience propels us to look for *my* way, what will bring *me* happiness, satisfaction, fulfilment. But the clear call of Jesus to each of us is to follow *the* Way. The Way, as we all know, is Jesus. He is the Way, the way that is truth and life.

It might seem to us that we are making no progress; it might seem to us that we've been saying the mantra for weeks, months, years, with no result. When you think that, remember this: It's not your way, it's *the* Way. The journey we are on is not just our journey, it is *the* Journey. The Way is Jesus; the Way is truth and life.

This is from the Gospel of Matthew:

> *'No one is worthy of me who does not take up his cross and walk in my footsteps. By gaining his life, a man will lose it; by losing his life for my sake, he will gain it'.* (Matt 10:38-39)

A little later in the same Gospel:

> *Jesus then said to his disciples, 'If anyone wishes to be a follower of mine, he must leave self behind; he must take up his cross and come with me. Whoever cares for his own safety is lost, but if a man will let himself be lost for my sake, he will find his true self. What will a man gain by winning the whole world, at the cost of his own true self? Or what can a man give that will buy that self back?'* (Matt 16:24-26)

6.9 The Ultimate Aim of Meditation

When you begin to meditate for the first time, most people find that right at the beginning they do come to a most extraordinary silence and peacefulness. But then as they proceed, this gives way to a very distracted state of being. They feel at that stage that "meditation is not for me, I have no talent for it; all I seem to get now when I meditate is more and more distractions". I think this is the moment to persevere.

The ultimate aim of meditation is to bring you to a total silence. It has to be a silence that is entirely unself-conscious. Now the way the ancient wisdom expressed this was: "The monk who knows he is praying is not praying; the monk who does not know he is praying is praying." So, as soon as you realize consciously that you are in this silence and it's very marvellous, you must begin to say your mantra immediately. That trains you in the generosity of not trying to possess the fruit of your meditation. This is difficult for people, because most people in our society get into most trips so that they can experience the experience. Meditation is different from that in that it is an entry into pure experience.

So you say your mantra until you come to a total silence, and you can be in that silence for a split second, for a minute, maybe twenty minutes; but, as soon as you realize you are in it, start saying the mantra again. And, don't try to make that happen. That's another hazard, that we want to make progress, that we want to get some kind of verification that the whole business of saying the mantra for five years is going to be worth it. At that stage, you must resist the temptation to want to possess the fruits of meditation. You must just meditate and say the mantra. When you realize you are not saying it, say it again.

But it's those moments of pure silence that are the moments of revelation. I don't often speak of this because it would be disastrous to try to confect that experience. No one listening to what we are saying here should ever try to confect that experience. What you must do is say your mantra, be content to say it, be humble to say it, be simple to say it. The gift of pure prayer, of pure contemplation, of pure silence, is an absolute gift, never something that we can earn or twist God's arm to get. When it's given, we accept it with joy, and then we say our mantra again.

7 THE FRUITS

Everyone who perseveres in meditation discovers that although during the time of meditation it might appear that nothing happens, yet gradually the whole of our life is changed.

John Main

7.1	Living in the Present Moment
7.2	Learning to Be
7.3	Abandonment of Desire
7.4	Detachment
7.5	Liberty of Spirit
7.6	Freedom
7.7	Growing in Love
7.8	Rooted in God
7.9	Personal Harmony
7.10	Mature Relationships
7.11	Christian Community
7.12	Other-Centredness
7.13	Meaning, Significance, and Purpose
7.14	Stability
7.15	Fullness of Life
7.16	Values System Based on God

7.1 Living in the Present Moment

What we do when we meditate is enter fully into the present moment. Each time you recite your mantra, you are wholly present to that moment.

To meditate, you have to learn to say the mantra from the beginning of your meditation until the end. Whatever thought comes to you, however brilliant, whatever idea, however original, let it go. Don't hang on to it. And listen to the sound of your mantra. What this leads us to is to an attention, a spirit of attention, a mindfulness of what *is*. Not what has been, and not what might be, but what *is*.

You are not thinking of the past; you are not planning for the future. You are there, totally, in that moment. Many of us, perhaps most of us, spend so much time thinking about the past or so much time planning for the future that for much of the time our minds can become easily distracted with memories and with plans. There is a very real danger that we will never come to terms fully with the present. I am sure all of you know how painful it is to be with someone who is always living in the past. It is equally painful to be with someone who is always thinking about the future.

To meditate, we have to learn to be wholly attentive to our mantra, to listen to it, with simplicity of spirit and with concentration. When we meditate we are not thinking about the past at all. In a real sense, we have become freed from the past. We are freed from the past because, as we meditate, as we open ourselves to the power of the living Christ, we realize that the past has no ultimate power over us because of the reality of what is, of now, of the present. Just as we are freed of the past, so we are freed of the future at that very moment when we realize that what *is*, is sufficient. It is sufficient for now, forever, for eternity.

When we meditate, we are not trying to make the present happen. We are not trying to make anything happen. The present is. We are not trying to conjure up God, or his power or his Spirit. God is. It is extremely important for us to know that when we meditate, we are simply being open to the present, to what is.

So the question that arises for us is, "What is?" To say that God is would be enough. But the power of the Christian revelation consists in its proclamation that God is, God is now, God is here, God is always, God is in our hearts, God is love. Wisdom in the Christian vision consists in having this truth sharply in focus, in knowing all this with utter certainty. It consists in living out of the power of this truth with every ounce of our energy, in every fibre of our being. It consists in the willingness to be transformed by that power, to be taken out of and beyond ourselves into the very heart of the Mystery itself. Christian meditation is the process whereby we reduce ourselves to that point of nothingness that allows this truth to enter us, to become wholly real for us.

By becoming wholly present in this moment, in the moment when we say the mantra, we enter into the *eternal now* of God.

7.2 Learning to Be

Meditation is a state of being where you are not thinking, you are not imagining, you are not having imaginary conversations with anyone. You are in perfect peace, in perfect stillness, in perfect quiet. In the silence of meditation, when you go beyond thought and imagination, you are learning to *be*. To be ourselves, not to be as it were defining ourselves by some activity, whether that activity is some work or some thinking process, but simply to *be*. To be the person you are, without trying to justify your existence or make excuses for your existence. Just to *be*, as you are.

The wonder of it is that the more simple you become, the more you are able to enjoy to the full the gift of your being. You have to let go of your thoughts, of your ideas, of your ambitions, and you have to *be*.

The way to do it is to say your word. If all your attention is directed to saying your word, gradually (and you have to be patient) you are unhooked from all the thoughts and words and ideas and hopes and fears. It is this liberation from the fear, the guilt, the ambition, that allows you to be who you are without having to justify yourself.

Every morning and every evening, you give yourself the opportunity to *be*, to be in utter simplicity, to be in humility. Not asking yourself, "What is happening to me now?" Not trying to analyse yourself, "Am I enjoying this? Am I getting anything out of this?" During this time of being, you put your self-reflective ego entirely aside.

We pass beyond all images, above all the image that we have of ourselves. We divest ourselves of all our masks. We as it were set them down on the ground beside us, and we begin to become the real person we are, in absolute simplicity. We are saying our mantra not to impress anyone; we are saying our mantra in order to leave all images, all words behind, so that we can be in utter simplicity.

When you meditate, you don't try to please anyone. You don't try to respond to any role or any image of yourself. In fact, when you are meditating, not only do you not try to respond to an image of yourself or someone else's image of yourself, but in meditating you let go of all images. You empty yourself. That is what meditating is about. It is the process of emptying out all the fantasy, all the images, all the unreality. That makes space for the real you, the real person you are. That's a way of looking at meditation. It is a way of making space for yourself to be.

Saying your mantra is a process of freedom. You are freeing yourself from the images, the fantasies, the memories that take away your freedom to be who you are. In the Christian vision of meditation, the whole purpose of this process is to free your spirit to be open to infinity, to allow your heart and your mind, your whole being, to expand beyond all the barriers of your own isolated self and to come into union with all. With the All; with God.

7.3 Abandonment of Desire

One thing we learn in meditation is to abandon desire. We learn it because we know that our invitation is to live wholly in the present moment. Reality is simply being grounded in God, the ground of our being. Desire demands constant movement, constant striving. Reality demands stillness and silence. That is the commitment that we make in meditating.

As each of you has found from your own experience, we learn in the stillness and silence to accept ourselves as we are. This sounds very strange to modern ears, above all to modern Christians who have been brought up to practise so much anxious striving: "Shouldn't I be ambitious? What if I'm a bad person, shouldn't I desire to be better?" The real tragedy of our time is that we are so filled with desire – for happiness, for success, for wealth, for power, whatever it may be – that we are always imagining ourselves as we *might* be. So we rarely come to know ourselves as we *are*, and we rarely come to accept our present position. It may well be that we are sinners, and if we are it is important that we should know that we are. But far more important for us is to know from our own experience that God is the ground of our being, and that we are rooted in him and founded in God. Each of us must know that personally, from our own experience, in our own hearts. This is the stability that we all need, not the striving and movement of desire but the stability and the stillness of rootedness. Each of us is invited to learn in our meditation, in our stillness in God, that in him we have all things that are necessary.

Prayer has very little to do with asking for this or asking for that. Prayer is something much more simple than that. It is being at one with God. Why is it so difficult? I think it is so difficult for us as men and women of the twentieth century because we live in such a materialistic society that sees everything in terms of possession and possessing.

Even if we happen to be more spiritual in our outlook, we can easily become spiritual materialists. Instead of accumulating money, we try to accumulate grace or merit. But the way of prayer is the way of dispossession and of surrender. That is hard for us because we have been taught success, we have been taught the importance of winning, not losing. But Jesus tells us that if we would find our life, we must lose it. Saying our mantra is exactly our response to that command of Jesus: to be wholly at his disposition, to give him our undivided attention, to give him our undivided heart, to be in the state of undivided consciousness, which is another way of saying to be at one with him.

We could perhaps describe prayer as the state of obediential love. The state wherein we are wholly at God's disposition, not desiring, not planning, but simply placing ourselves within the fullness of his gift of life, the fullness of his gift of our own unique creation. Each one of us in this room is created for a unique destiny, a unique fulfilment in God. Our only task in life is to be wholly open to that destiny. Our task is to live out of the divine energy, to live within the divine plan, and to play our part in it fully and generously.

Meditation does call for that abandonment of desire and desiring. Positively, it calls for generous openness to God's destiny for us, to his plan for us, to his love for us. What you discover in meditation is just that – his love for you.

The mantra is like the needle of a compass. It heads you always in the direction of your own destiny. It points always to the true direction you must follow, away from self into God. Whichever way your ego may lead you, the compass is always faithful in the direction it points you in. The mantra, if you say it with generosity, with faithfulness, and with love, will always point you in the direction of God.

7.4 Detachment

One of the most important lessons that meditation has to teach us is detachment. Detachment is not dissociation from yourself, turning away from your own problems or your own life situation. It is not a denial of friendship or affection, or even of passion. Detachment is, in essence, detachment from self-preoccupation, from that mind-set that puts *me* at the centre of all creation.

Detachment is concerned with friendship, with true brotherhood and sisterhood, with true love. True friendship and true love is only possible if we are detached from our own self-preoccupation, self-isolation, from our own self-indulgence. The disengagement that detachment involves is from using other people for one's own ends. But above all, detachment is liberation from the anxiety we have about our own survival as a self.

Detachment is the state we enter into in our meditation, a state wherein we are not possessed by our possessions, where we are not dominated by the desire to possess, to control – a state of mind, a way of being that is absolutely necessary if we are going to love. Because in this state of detachment, we do not try to possess or to control the other. We do not try to remake the other in our own image and likeness. But we allow the other to be. And allowing them to be, we know them as they are. And knowing them, we love them. In meditating, we let go of our desire to control, to possess, to dominate. We seek to be who we are. Being who we are, we are open to the God who is. It is in that openness that we are filled with wonder, with power, with energy – the energy to be, and to be in love. Entering into this state requires of us great generosity, the generosity to let go of our plans, of our hopes, of our fears, at the time of meditation so that we may be detached enough to be ourselves at all times. Detached enough to see beyond ourselves, to see who God is. And seeing, to be in love.

The way to this detachment is the way of the mantra. It is the mantra and our faithfulness to it that loosens within us the roots of the ego that constantly leads us back into desire. In God's time, the root is so loosened that it is plucked out.

To be detached from our possessions is to be free from our possessions – to possess them, if necessary, yet not be possessed by them. In many ways it is easy enough to be detached from our material possessions. In meditation we have to learn a more demanding detachment. We must learn a detachment not only from our thoughts, our feelings, our desires, but even from our self-consciousness. This not only seems to our modern minds to be an impossibility, but it even seems to be a scandal that anybody should seriously propose this. But this is exactly the truth. It is the truth proclaimed by Jesus and the truth lived by the saints and sages down through the ages.

Loving is in essence losing oneself in the larger reality of the other, of others, and of God. Detachment from self-centredness liberates us for love. We are no longer dominated by the quest for survival. Detachment requires trust: trust of the other, trust of others, trust in God. It requires the willingness to let go, to give up controlling, and to be. The commitment in meditation is to be sufficiently detached from self-conscious preoccupation, by the commitment to the mantra and the daily commitment to it. Our times of meditation become progressively more simple, more joyous, more centred. You understand in meditation, from your own experience, what it means to say, "God is love."

Listen to the words of Jesus:

Whoever cares for his own safety is lost; but if a man will let himself be lost for my sake, he will find his true self.
(Matt 16:25)

To meditate is to lose yourself, to become absorbed in God, to be utterly lost in the generous immensity that we call God.

7.5 Liberty of Spirit

One of the things that I suppose everybody searches for in their life is to discover a real liberty of spirit. We are constrained by so many things – by fear and by trying to project the image of ourselves that we feel others expect. I think people suffer a great deal of frustration because they cannot be themselves and cannot make contact with themselves.

Now what Jesus came to proclaim was precisely this liberty. The liberty to be ourselves and the liberty to find ourselves in him, through him and with him. Meditation is the way to that liberty. It is the way to your own heart. It is the way to the depth of your own being, where you can simply *be* – not justify yourself, not apologize for yourself, but simply rejoice in the gift of your own being.

What is this liberty of spirit? I think all of us know deep down that we have this call to liberty, that we have this capacity for liberty. All of us know that we cannot live our lives to the full if we are always trapped in trivia, if we are always absorbed in things that are passing away. Now when we think of liberty, we tend to think of the freedom to do what we want to do. Certainly this is an element in all living. But the liberty of spirit of which the New Testament speaks is not just freedom to *do*. It is above all the freedom, the liberty, to *be* – to be who we are, to be one, all our potentialities joined together in a deep personal harmony. The liberty that the New Testament speaks of is a liberty to enter into our own personal and unique relationship with the One who is, with God. It's the liberty to discover that this unique and personal relationship to which each of us is summoned, the relationship with the One, is our relationship with all. What we are invited to discover in our lives – and each one of us must make sure that we don't just let our lives slip through our hands – what we are invited to discover is our personal harmony, the unique gift of our own creation, and the potentiality that we all have to enter into harmony with the One, with all.

7.6 Freedom

Everybody wants to be free. But there are various ways of understanding freedom. Perhaps the biggest understanding of it that people of our time have is freedom from domination by someone else, by some other country. We tend to look at freedom in terms of our own escape from domination. One of the things that Jesus has to say to all of us is that freedom is ours. Freedom is the most precious gift given to each of us, but not merely to escape domination. Freedom is freedom for being. Perhaps the most important thing in the lives of each one of us is that we should be free to be ourselves, to respond to the gift of our own creation. In the Christian vision each of us is invited to experience what St Paul called the 'liberty of the children of God'. Not freedom *from* but freedom *for* – for life, for your own life, for the fullness of your life and of all life in Christ.

Meditation is simply a way of entering into this freedom. It is the freedom that each of us can find if only we will undertake the discipline of the journey.

But as soon as we hear the word discipline, we feel, "Isn't this a loss of freedom?" We cannot help approaching meditation saying, "Okay, I'll try it, I'll see if there's anything in it for me. If there is, I'll stick with it; if there isn't, I'll give it up and try jogging or something else." We cannot approach meditation in that way. That's the challenge it presents to us as modern people because we are not used to doing something unless there is a pay-off.

Freedom is not just freedom from things. Christian liberty is not just freedom from desire, from sin. We are free for intimate union with God, which is another way of saying we are free for infinite expansion of spirit in God. Meditation is to enter into that experience of being free for God, transcending desire, sin, ego, leaving it behind so that the whole of our being is utterly available to God. It is in that profound availability that we become ourselves.

Listen to these words of Jesus:

Turning to the Jews who had believed in him, Jesus said, 'If you dwell within the revelation I have brought, you are indeed my disciples; you shall know the truth, and the truth will set you free.' (John 8:31-2)

Meditation is simply dwelling within the revelation, dwelling within the vision of God.

7.7 Growing in Love

Everyone who perseveres in meditation discovers that although during our time of meditation it might appear that nothing happens, yet gradually the whole of our life is changed. We have to be patient; we might like it to be changed more rapidly. Our thought becomes clarified, relationships become more loving. This is because, in the process of meditation, we are made free *to* love *by* Love. The reason for all this is really very simple. When we meditate, not only do we stand back from the individual operations of our being, but we begin to learn to find a wholly new ground to stand on. We discover a rootedness of being. The rootedness is not just in ourselves, but we discover ourselves rooted in God. Rooted in God who is Love.

The peace, the stillness and the harmony that we experience in meditation becomes the basis for all our action. All our judgments are now illumined, inspired by love, because we know that that love is the very ground of our being. All this happens because we learn the courage to take the attention off ourselves. We learn to stop thinking about ourselves. We allow ourselves to *be* – to be still, to be silent. And in that stillness and silence we find ourselves in God, in love.

What you will find is that the experience itself is self-authenticating. You will find that the more you meditate, the more your day seems to come into shape and the more purpose you have in your life. Then, the more you begin to see the meaning in everything and the more you will find that love grows in your heart. Now it may be that there is a good deal of meanness there as well, but the love is growing. That is the real test of meditation. But you cannot put any sort of materialistic test to meditation, like "Do I get fantastic visions when I meditate?" The real test is the love growing in your heart.

A couple of years ago, a man came to our Monday evening group. Each Monday evening, he would ask the same question. He would say: "How long do I have to keep this up for? I have been meditating for three, four months every morning and every evening, and absolutely nothing is happening. It's all very well for you to sit there and say that I've got to have no expectations, that I've got to accept the discipline of it , that I've got to have faith. But, surely to God, something has got to happen one day."

Now that went on until one evening he wasn't there. As everyone was leaving, at about half past nine, he turned up. I could see that something had happened to him. There were smiles all over his face. "An extraordinary thing has just happened," he said. "As I was turning the corner at the bottom of the hill to come up here, a young kid pushed his bike in front of my car. I could see that he did it deliberately. I just tapped it and stopped. Immediately, three kids surrounded the car and demanded, 'You've got to pay me compensation; you've wrecked my bike.' I was amazed how calm I was. I said, 'Let's get the bike into the car and we'll drive round to the police station.'" He had some job persuading them but eventually he got them around and took them in. He said that throughout the whole thing he was simply amazed at his calm attitude towards this experience.

What he said to me was: "Well, you know, I don't suppose anything is ever going to happen in my meditation, but I do see that it's going to change my life!"

Now, that's the experience of all of us who meditate. The great test as to whether your meditation is working, or whether you are making progress (I don't advise you to rate yourselves) is: Are you growing in love; are you growing in patience; are you growing in understanding and compassion? That is the effect of our meditation. With some of us, it takes longer. With some of us, the end of egoism requires a big struggle. Sometimes, we are carried more or less kicking and screaming into the Kingdom of Heaven.

But the important thing is not to bother how long it takes. It doesn't matter how long it takes. The only thing that matters — and the thing that I wish I could communicate to everyone here this evening — the only thing that matters is that we are on the journey. The journey is a journey away from self, away from egoism, away from selfishness, away from isolation. It's a journey into the infinite love of God.

7.8 Rooted in God

There are all sorts of extravagant claims made for the benefits of meditating. You can hear it said that if you work for a large organization meditating will help you get on better with the boss. Or I suppose, if you happen to be the boss, it will help you better to get on with your secretary. All these claims are put forward because we are so materialistic in our society that it is very difficult for us to realize that there is something in life that is worth doing in itself, without any pay-off.

Why meditation is so important for us is that it does help us to live our lives as a process of growth, that we live our lives in a constant, deepening maturity. Nothing I suppose is sadder than a person who lives their life, and somehow never grows up, never benefits by their experience.

Meditation is important because it leads you to that first step in all growth, which is rootedness. By meditating every morning and every evening, you set out on that way of rootedness, becoming rooted in your own deepest, innermost centre. In our society all sorts of helps are given to us to grow intellectually. Not so many helps are given to us to grow spiritually, to make contact with our own deepest personal centre and to begin to live our lives out of that centre, not being blown around by every wind that happens to come up on the surface, but to be rooted in ourselves.

Growth also needs cultivation. Meditation, because of its highly practical orientation, leads us day in and day out to return to that centre, to return to that rootedness in ourselves.

Meditation is a process of growing, of growing more spiritually aware. Like all processes of growth, it has its own speed, its own pace. It is an organic process. You have, as it were, to root the mantra in your heart. As you know, Jesus often spoke of the Word of the

Gospel taking root in the hearts of men and women. He tells us it has to fall into good soil. In other words, the whole of your being has to be involved in this process. You sound the mantra. And by your fidelity in returning to it day after day, you root it in your heart. Once rooted, it flourishes. Indeed it flowers. The flower of meditation is peace, a profound peace. It is a peace that arises from harmony, from the dynamic harmony that you encounter when you make contact with the ground of your being. What you discover is that the mantra is rooted in your heart in the centre of your being, and your being is rooted in God, the centre of all being. You find yourself in God. Finding yourself in God, you come to understanding that your life is a gift, that you offer it back to God. The gift that was a finite gift when it was given to you becomes, in the offering back, an infinite gift.

7.9 Personal Harmony

To discover our essential harmony and wholeness, which is what finding oneself means, we cannot concentrate on just one limited part of our being.

By personal harmony, I mean the integration, the perfect co-operation of mind and heart, body and spirit. I am a whole person and I respond wholly. We know that we are this whole person, this harmony, and yet we do not know it because this knowledge has not yet become fully conscious. Perhaps we can say that this conscious harmony that lives in perfect joy and liberty at the centre of our being has not yet expanded and spread itself throughout our being.

To allow it to do so, we must simply remove the obstacle of narrowly self-conscious thought, self-important language. In other words, we must become silent. If a man really did know himself as body-mind-spirit, as the harmony of these three, then he would be on the way to making that knowledge fully conscious throughout his whole being.

We are not just an extreme of body and an extreme of mind co-existing. We have a principle of unity within our being, in the centre of our being. It is this: our spirit, which is the image of God within us.

Listen to the fourteenth century author of *The Cloud of Unknowing*:

> *I tell you the truth when I say that this work [of meditation] demands great serenity, an integrated and pure disposition in soul and body ... God forbid that I should separate what God has coupled: the body and the spirit.* (ch 41, 48)

The way to become fully conscious of this essential harmony of our being is to be silent. And to meditate is to be silent. The harmony of our essence, our centre, then, as it were blossoms and diffuses itself throughout every part and molecule of our being. *The Cloud of Unknowing* puts it very charmingly:

> *When grace draws a man to contemplation, it seems to transfigure him even physically so that though he may be ill-favoured by nature he now appears changed and lovely to behold.* (ch 54)

The diffusion of our essential harmony throughout our being is another way of saying that the prayer of the Spirit of Jesus wells up in our hearts, floods our hearts and overflows throughout us. This is the amazing gift we have been given by Jesus sending us his Spirit. "Do you not know," wrote St Paul to the Corinthians, "that your body is a shrine of the indwelling Holy Spirit, and that that Spirit is God's gift to you?" (1 Cor 6:19) But he does not force it on us. It is for us to recognize it and to accept it. This we do, not by being clever or self-analytical, but by being silent, by being simple. The gift is already given. We have merely to open our hearts to its infinite generosity. The mantra opens our hearts in pure simplicity.

7.10 Mature Relationships

Meditation is a way to mature human relationships.

We tend to think of prayer as a somewhat individual activity, and our involvement with the community as something else. But in the New Testament, there is one central unifying reality. That is the reality of love: love of God, love of neighbour, love of ourselves. Jesus is the revelation of God. In the New Testament, he is God's love made visible in the world. His vision is a vision of a community of brethren. Christianity, in the vision of Jesus, is a fellowship of brothers and sisters who respond together to the same reality that is beyond them and yet contains them and constantly expands them.

In our meditation, we seek to *be*, to be who we are, and to come into the presence of God who is as he is. Above all, we know that in our prayer, we are not trying to possess God or to change him. We are trying to be one with him as he is.

There is a new and wonderful dimension added to prayer when we can find brethren with whom we can share this experience. In sharing our meditation together, we similarly accept one another as we are. We are not trying to possess one another or to change one another. Each of us seeks to *be*, to the fullest of our potential. What we know, both from the words of Jesus and from our experience of him in our own hearts, is that to *be* in the Christian vision is to be *with* and to be *for*. The wonderful thing about the community that is built for those who pray together is that we find people to be *with* and people who are *for* us.

So meditation is a way to mature human relationships, relationships that enable us to really rejoice in the being of another, with no wish to possess or control them, but simply to know the other as he or she is, and to delight in that knowing. And it is the same with God. We don't set out to harass him, to bombard him with words, to demand that he takes notice of us, to demand that he reveals himself to us, on our own terms. In the simplicity of our meditation, in the simplicity of our humble repetition of the mantra, we seek solely to be with him, to be for him, to rejoice in being with him, and to be more and more profoundly at one with him.

In the journey of meditation, as we say our mantra and we let go of our thoughts and plans and ideas and imaginings, we learn the value of renunciation, of non-possessiveness. We let go of our own images of self; we let go of our own desires; we let go of our own fears and of our own self-consciousness. This renunciation enables us to enter into communion with the other, and with others, at a deep level of reality.

The solitude of our meditation is the foundation stone on which we build all communion, true communion with ourselves, with others and with God. It's in the silence of our own heart that we enter into the deep harmony that reveals to us our oneness with all.

Listen to St Paul writing to the Colossians:

> *Put on the garments that suit God's chosen people, his own, his beloved, and those garments are compassion, kindness, humility, gentleness, patience. Be forbearing with one another and forgiving where any of you has cause for complaint: you must forgive as the Lord forgave you. To crown all, there must be love, to bind all together and to complete the whole. Let Christ's peace be arbiter in your hearts, for to this peace you were all called as members of a single body. (Col 3:12-15)*

7.11 Christian Community

Our Christian communities do not exist for themselves, but for others and ultimately for the Other. The very essence of our meaning is to exist for others.

The Church does not exist to perpetuate itself, to guard itself against injury, to increase its own security. It exists to lead others into an awareness of the redemptive love of God in Jesus.

> *'You are light for all the world...'* [Jesus told his disciples].
> *'When a lamp is lit, it is not put under the meal tub, but on the lamp-stand where it gives light to everyone in the house. And you, like the lamp, must shed light among your fellows, so that, when they see the good you do, they may give praise to your Father in Heaven.'* (Matt 5:14–16)

There is only one way to do this. This is the way of prayer. In our prayer, we have to discover ourselves existing for the Other, because it is in prayer that we experience ourselves being created and sustained by him.

In our prayer, we let God be; we rejoice in his being as he is. We do not try to manipulate him, to harangue him or to flatter him; we do not dispel him with our clever words and formulae. But, we worship him, that is we acknowledge his value and worth. In doing this, we discover that we, created in his image, share in his value and worth as children of God.

But there is also something in all of us that incites us to control the other. The crime of idolatry is, precisely, creating our own god, in our own image and likeness. Rather than encounter God in his awesome difference from ourselves, we construct a toy model of him in our own psychic and emotional image. In doing this, we do not harm him, of course, as unreality has no power over God. But we do debase and scatter ourselves, surrendering the potential and divine glory of our humanity for the false glitter of the golden calf.

The truth is so much more exciting, so much more wonderful. God is not a reflection of our consciousness but we are his reflection and image by our incorporation with Jesus, God's Son, our Brother.

Our way to the experience of this truth is in the silence of our meditation. The power that silence has is to allow this truth to emerge, to rise to the surface, to become visible. We know that it is greater than we are, and we find a perhaps unexpected humility within ourselves that leads us to real attentive silence. We let the truth be.

Just as we can cut God down to our own size, impose our identity on him, so we can do this with other people. In meditation, we develop our capacity to turn our whole being towards the Other. We learn to let our neighbour be, just as we learn to let God be. We learn not to manipulate our neighbour but rather to reverence him, to reverence his importance, the wonder of his being. In other words, we learn to love him.

Because of this, prayer is the great school of community. In and through a common seriousness and perseverance in prayer, we realize the true glory of Christian community as a fraternity of the anointed, living together in profound and loving mutual respect.

Christian community is in essence the experience of being held in reverence by others, and we in our turn reverencing them. In others, I recognize the same Spirit that lives in my heart, the Spirit that constitutes my real self. In this recognition of the other person, a recognition that remakes our minds and expands our consciousness, the other person comes into being as he really is, in his real self, not as a manipulated extension of myself. He moves and acts out of his own integral reality and no longer as some image created by my imagination. Even if our ideas or principles clash, we are held in unison by our mutual recognition of each other's infinite lovableness, importance and essential unique reality.

True community happens in the process of drawing each other into the light of true being. In this process, we share a deepening experience of the joy of life, the joy of *being*, as we discover more and more of its fullness in a loving faith shared with others. The essence of community then is a recognition of and deep reverence for the other.

Our meditation partakes of this essence because it leads us to turn wholly towards the Other, who is the Spirit in our heart. So complete is our attention to the other that we say nothing ourselves but wait for the other to speak. The mantra guides us into a deeper consciousness of the silence that reigns within us, and then supports us while we wait.

7.12 Other-Centredness

For St Paul the heart of the Christian mystery is the presence of the Divine energy in our ordinary world. This is the mystery hidden at the centre of everything. The Christian revelation is that this energy, the basic energy of all life, is Love.

In baptism we are baptized into a community of love. The basic unit in that community of love is the family because it is there we all receive our first experience of the full warmth of human love and care. It is there we have the first, foundational experiences that allow us later to recognize the full meaning of "God is love." (1 John 4:9)

It is the power of love that informs and transforms us at the centre of our whole being. Love grows and develops in the human heart. "God's love has flooded our inmost heart through the Holy Spirit he has given us" (Rom 5:5) because we are all loved in the sacred, incarnate, human, heart of Jesus.

Each person does not become the full person they are called to be except in a relationship of love. And to love is to be other-centred. Paul, then, places Christianity right at the centre of the life experience of the majority of people, in marriage.

How precisely does marriage incarnate the Christian mystery of love? And why is our earliest experience of life in the family so important? The answer in both cases is 'other-centredness'. To love is to be other-centred. The vision of love proclaimed by Jesus is the vision of transcendence, that is being taken beyond ourselves through the Son in the Spirit to the Father. In the preaching of Jesus himself it is always evident that his centre of consciousness is in the Father, and from this derives both his authority, his power and his effective meaning for man. His other-centredness involves us and challenges us, because, as a result of his being centred in the Father, he is centred also in us. As St John reports: "As the Father has loved me, so I have loved you. Dwell in my love. If you heed my commandments, you will dwell in my love, as I have heeded my Father's commands and dwell in his love." (John 15:9-10) His commandment, as we know, is to love one another.

His love for the Father and the Father's love for him is intimately connected with the love of a married couple and their children. The common movement in both cases is the movement away from self to the other. To love is to be other-centred.

The other-centredness of love, a love that will transform us in Christ, will present a real challenge to the self-centredness, the egoism of most of us. And so Paul urges, "Give yourselves wholly to prayer" (Eph 6:18), prayer that is rooted in the power of the Spirit.

Marriage and prayer are intimately related in Paul's vision of the Christian life. Their common dynamic is the connection of other-centredness to union, two interdependent features of love. But it is not union itself that is sought as an end but the other, in and for him or her self. Union then takes place naturally because, Paul tells us, we seek the other, love the other. And the result of this is something greater than mere individuality alone: "and the two become a single body' (Eph 5:31). St Paul writes, "There is one body and one Spirit" and we are "all of us the parts of one body". (Eph 4.4, 4:25)

Reflect on what St Paul understands as the result of union. His union with Christ led him to write, "I live now no longer but Christ lives in me" (Gal 2:20). This experience that underlies all his writings is squarely based on the words of Jesus himself on which the whole Christian gospel is based: "No man can be a follower of mine unless he leaves self behind" (Mark 8:34). "By gaining his life a man will lose it; by losing his life for my sake, he will gain it." (Matt 10:39)

In both prayer and marriage the call is to full selfhood by loss of self in the other. In prayer, as in marriage, the giving of self must become total because the surrender called for is to a reality beyond us and greater than us. Both prayer and marriage are creative of life because of the generosity and faith that enable us to lay down our lives in love.

The fullness of this experience of love is only disclosed to us in silence. A loving marriage is often revealed by the capacity of the couple to remain in confident, positive silence with each other. In prayer, too, it is the silence of love that leads us into the mystery of Christ when we are with the other in the deep stillness of loving acceptance.

7.13 Meaning, Significance, and Purpose

We, all of us, know that we can't live a full life unless our life is firmly grounded on some underlying purpose, unless we come to know that each of us has an ultimate significance. That ultimate significance we can only discover if we find our essential rootedness, our rootedness in God.

It's as though we were rushing through our lives, and in our hearts there is the flame of a candle. Because we are moving at such high speed, this essential interior flame is always on the point of going out. But when we sit down to meditate, when we become still, when we are not thinking in terms of our success or self-importance, of our own will, when we are just still in the presence of the One who *is*, then the flame begins to burn brightly. We begin to understand ourselves and others in terms of light, warmth and love.

Now we have to get to that point where we can learn to be still. That is why we say our word, our mantra. Saying the mantra leads us to this stillness where the flame of being can burn bright.

It is so easy to let our lives just become mere routine. It's so easy for us just to play some role, whether it be student, mother, husband, manager, monk, or whatever. But Jesus came to tell us that life is not about playing roles, or being a functionary in some system. Life is about meaning, significance and purpose. The message of Jesus to each of us is that every one of us has personal meaning, significance, value and importance. That value that each of us possesses arises from who we are, in ourselves. It doesn't arise from what anyone else or society says we are.

The message of Jesus to each one of us is that we must discover that fundamental and basic truth about ourselves. We must discover our rootedness in God. We must be open to the love that redeems us. We must live out of our own infinite holiness;

each of us is a temple of the Holy Spirit. The Spirit of him who created the universe dwells in our hearts, and in silence is loving to all. We must discover that, and we must discover that for ourselves and live out of it personally.

In the sort of society we live in, we have to take radical steps. We live in a society that does not recognize the immense value of spiritual practice or the spiritual reality.

Meditation is a way that enables us each day to root our lives in the divine reality of God. It is a positive way. It isn't a way in which we, as it were, reject the world or build any false opposition to the world. We wish to live our lives fully in the world. We can only do that if we have the confidence that comes from rootedness in God.

To learn to meditate is quite a demand. It means that we must give time to the most important fact in life. The most important fact of life is that God is, and that his Spirit dwells in our hearts. We need to start our day out of the power of God's presence within us. We need to bring our day to a conclusion returning to the mystery of his presence, of his love.

Meditation is a way that brings every part of our being, of our lives, of our experience, into harmony. Meditation is the way beyond dividedness, beyond the dividedness that we so often experience within ourselves. It's the way across the divide that separates us from God. It's the way to deep peace and to joy.

7.14 Stability

We live in a world that makes great demands on most of us. In every society now, stress and strain take their toll on the nervous resources of so many people.

One of the qualities that we as monks have tried to respond to is what St Benedict calls 'stability'. In the Rule, St Benedict gives this stability as one of the principal objectives in the life of the person who would live their Christianity to the full. To be stable we need to be sure of ourselves. We need to be sure that we are standing on firm ground. We need to be sure, confident, that we would not be blown away by the first storm winds that come up.

Meditation is a way to this stability, the stability which is the reality of our own being. What each of us needs is to be firmly anchored in our own reality.

Saying the mantra is like dropping the anchor, anchoring yourself in the depths of your own being. We have to go down below the surface into the depths of our being. For many of us, this is an unfamiliar experience. We are so caught up in dealing with all that is happening on the surface that we don't have the time to stand aside from surface concerns to go down to the depths. Once we touch the ground of our own being, we make an extraordinary discovery. Final rootedness, real stability for each of us can only come when we are firmly anchored in God. The extraordinary discovery that is there for us all to make is that, once we are anchored in ourselves, we are anchored in God. This is a great discovery to make because it is at the same time a discovery of our own fragility; we can so easily be tossed around by the storms of life. But it is at the same time a discovery of our own extraordinary potential: to become one with the energy of God, and with his energy and his power to expand our lives, ourselves, into generosity, into love, and into life, into eternal life, which is to say limitless life.

We must be anchored in God. We must be with him in his presence. To come into that presence, we have first to be wholly present to ourselves. This is where we begin. Learning to be present to ourselves as we say the mantra and nothing but the mantra, we learn to dwell in God.

Listen to Jesus:

> *He who dwells in me, as I dwell in him, bears much fruit; for apart from me you can do nothing... If you dwell in me, and my words dwell in you, ask what you will, and you shall have it. This is my Father's glory, that you may bear fruit in plenty and so be my disciples. As the Father has loved me, so I have loved you. Dwell in my love. If you heed my commands, you will dwell in my love, as I have heeded my Father's commands and dwell in his love.* (John 15:5, 7-10)

That's an excellent description of meditation: To dwell, to abide, to remain in the love of God.

7.15 Fullness of Life

The most important thing for all of us is to live our lives to the full; insofar as we can, to realize our own full potential. Meditation is important for us because it is the process whereby we keep our contact with the creative centre of our being not just open but in a constant and continuous state of expansion. Meditation is a process whereby creative energy is released within us.

In our modern secular world, we easily forget that we have a divine origin, a divine source; that the incandescent energy of our own spirit emanates from the Spirit of God. We forget that God is our Creator. In the forgetting, we lose contact with our own essential nature. Because we lose this sense of contact with our divine origin, we ourselves become dehumanized.

It's so easy for us to become dehumanized, to become just consumers in a materialistic, commercial society. It's so easy to live our lives in some sort of mechanical way, going through routines each day, but losing the sense of freshness, of creativity, of freedom. As a result, we live our lives in a sort of rush, one routine following the next, distracted perhaps for a bit by entertainment, by pleasure, or deadened by the pressures of work or play.

Now this evening, I want to put before you two things that we must do if we want to break out of this cycle.

First, each one of us has to learn to stop the rush of activity. We must learn the priority of being. We must learn to be still. That's what our regular times of meditation are about.

The second thing that we have to learn is to be profoundly silent. We have to learn to stop the racket going on around us and in our head. It's easy enough to switch off the radio, the television or the stereo. But it is not so easy to switch off the multiplicity of ideas and imagination going on within our own heads. That's the purpose of saying the mantra.

Meditation addresses both of these problems. We learn to be still, and we learn to be silent. In learning to be still, we learn to be in our own place, to be rooted in our own place. The place for us to be is to be found within ourselves. There's nothing our modern world needs more urgently than men and women who are rooted in themselves, confident of their own being, confident of their own capacity for goodness, their own capacity for loving and for being loved. For that confidence, we need that sense of being wholly at one with ourselves. Sitting still, every morning and every evening, we learn stillness and rootedness. Once we are rooted, once we are still, we begin the next great task – to learn to be attentive. We learn to be attentive to the mystery at the heart of creation, and we learn to live our lives in harmony with that mystery.

Listen to St John writing in his first letter:

> *Dear friends, let us love one another, because love is from God. Everyone who loves is a child of God and knows God, but the unloving know nothing of God. For God is love; and his love was disclosed to us in this, that he sent his only Son into the world to bring us life.* (1 John 4:7-9)

Our meditation is an entry into that fullness of life, rooted in ourselves, rooted in love, rooted in God.

7.16 Values System Based on God

To learn to meditate, we have to be prepared to enter into the whole truth: the truth about ourselves, the truth about others and the ultimate truth of all reality. For much of our life, we keep in place all sorts of filters that filter the truth as we allow it to come in and as we allow it to go out. Probably these filters are necessary for most of us as long as we are living our lives at the surface level, as long as we are trying by the expending of much energy to protect our own image of ourselves and to project our own image of ourselves.

Why do we build these protective defences around ourselves? It is, I suppose, because we are not sure whether other people will accept us as we are. Probably the reason for this is that we do not accept ourselves as we are. So our fears about ourselves must be dissolved.

The truly spiritual man or woman is the man or woman who is in harmony with everyone they meet. You meet people not on the basis of competition or of projecting any image to them of who you might be or would like to be or think you ought to be. You begin to meet everyone as you are, the person you are, comfortable, accepting of your own being. You accept it because, in the silence of your meditation, you come to the knowledge that you are accepted. It is not just that you are acceptable because you have done all the right things. What you discover as you begin to explore that basic relationship of creature-Creator is that you are accepted. In the Christian vision of meditation you discover something more. You discover in that silence that you are loved, that you are lovable. That is the discovery that everyone must make in their lives if they are going to become fully themselves, fully human.

In the vision proclaimed by Jesus you begin to know what St John meant when he said, "God is love." The extraordinary thing is (and this is again what I personally would like to be able to convey, to communicate, to everyone I meet) that love is to be found in your own heart.

This is an astonishing truth. In the hearts of each one of us, in the depths of our being, is to be found the source of endless, infinite love. This is the love that casts out all our fears. In casting it out, it enables us to become ourselves, to be the person we are called to be, to abandon all our images and all our defences. To become ourselves, we have simply to put ourselves in full contact with this power, with this energy that we call love.

Our spirit is expanding. Our heart is opening, we are becoming more generous. And the change in us comes about because, in meditation, we encounter the power to make this change possible. All of us would presumably like to be more kind, more understanding, more selfless, more sympathetic, more compassionate and so on. But, at the same time, we recognize ourselves as weak, mortal, fallible, human beings.

What we discover in meditation is the power source to enable us to live this way, and we discover that this power source is established right at the centre of our own being, in our own hearts. This is so because our order of values is changed. Instead of our value system being based on the self, on the ego, on success or self-promotion, or whatever, our values system becomes based on God. We discover in the revelation that takes place in our own hearts, the revelation that takes place as we discover the presence of Jesus there, that God is love. This brings us to the conclusion that unleashes great power – that there is only one thing that matters ultimately and that is that we grow in love. Everything else is secondary. Everything else is consequential. Once this insight becomes powerful enough, our lives become altered. We see the importance of compassion, of understanding. We begin to become really sensitive people who are in touch with life at its centre.

Remember, God is the centre, God is love, and Jesus is the revelation of this love.

Everyone who perseveres in meditation discovers that, although during our time of meditation it might appear that nothing happens, yet gradually the whole of our life is changed. We have to be patient, because we might like it to be changed more rapidly. Our relationships become more loving. This is because, in the process of meditation, we are made free to love by love.

8 THE WAY

The summons we have from Jesus is to follow the Way, not my way, but The Way. He is the Way, the way that is truth and life.

John Main

8.1	The Way of Silence
8.2	The Way of Stillness
8.3	The Way of Simplicity
8.4	The Way of Discipline
8.5	The Way of Commitment
8.6	The Way of Leaving Self Behind
8.7	The Way of Faith
8.8	The Way of Trust
8.9	The Way of Love
8.10	The Way of Wisdom
8.11	The Way of Enlightenment
8.12	The Way of Peace
8.13	The Way of Attention

8.1 The Way of Silence

Silence is the essential human response to the mystery of God, to the infinity of God.

It is as though the mystery of God is a wonderful multi-faceted diamond. When we talk about God or we think about God, it is as though we are responding to one or other of his facets. But when we are silent in his presence, we respond to the mystery which we call God as a whole, and that, omni-dimensionally. The wonder of it is that it is the whole of us that responds to the entirety of the mystery of God. It is not just our intellect, not just our emotions, not just the religious side of us or the secular side of us. Everything that we are responds to everything that he is, in absolute harmony, in absolute love. That is what the experience of Christian prayer is – our union with the one who is One.

How is this possible? It is possible through the Incarnate Reality that is Jesus. God is fully revealed in Jesus, fully present in Jesus, and the love of Jesus has made us one with him. By becoming open in silence to his reality, we become open in wonder to the reality of God. We learn to be silent by being content to say our mantra in humble fidelity.

To tread the spiritual path, we must learn to be silent. What is required of us is a journey into profound silence. Part of the problem of the weakening of religion in our times is that religion uses words for its prayers and rituals, but those words have to be charged with meaning. And they can only be charged with meaning sufficient to move our hearts, to set us out in new directions, to change our lives, if they spring from spirit. And spirit requires silence. We all need to use words, but to use them with power, we all need to be silent. Meditation is the way to silence, the way of silence. It is the way of the mantra, the word that leads us to such a silence that ultimately charges all words with meaning.

Silence is really absolutely necessary for the human spirit if it really is to thrive. Not only just to thrive, but to be creative, to have a creative response to life, to our environment, to our friends. Because the silence gives our spirit room to breathe, room to *be*. In silence, you don't have to be justifying yourself, apologizing for yourself, trying to impress anyone. You just have to be. It's a most marvellous experience when you come to it. The wonder of it is that, in that experience, you are completely free. You are not trying to play any role; you are not trying to fulfil anyone's expectations.

To learn to meditate, you have to learn to be silent, and not to be afraid of silence. One of the great problems for modern people is that we are so unused to silence. Many people live with a constant background of radio, or television, or some sort of noise going on. Now in meditation, you are, as it were, crossing over the threshold from the background noise into silence. Now let me just try to explain to you the reaction you must try to have to the silence. What happens is this. You begin to recite your word and you begin to feel more peaceful, more silent. Then you become aware that you are on the threshold of silence. This is sort of a critical moment for many people, because you are leaving the familiar world of your sounds, your ideas, your thoughts, and your words. You are crossing over into silence, and you don't know what's in store for you. That's why it is so important, so useful, to meditate in a group. That's why it is so important and so useful to meditate in a tradition that says to you, "Fear not, don't be afraid." The purpose of our meditation is to be in the presence of love, the love that, as Jesus tells us, casts out all fear. But it is a critical moment. Because if you go back to your thoughts, to your ideas, even perhaps to your prayers, you've turned away from the entry into silence, into prayer, into love.

I think what all of us have to learn is not so much that we have to create silence. The silence is there, within us. What we have to do is to enter into it, to become silent, to become the silence.

The purpose of meditation and the challenge of meditation is to allow ourselves to become silent enough to allow this interior silence to emerge. Silence is the language of the spirit.

Learning to say your mantra, learning to say your word, leaving behind all other words, ideas, imaginations and fantasies, is learning to enter into the presence of the Spirit who dwells in our inner heart, who dwells there in love. The Spirit of God dwells in our hearts in silence. In humility and in faith, we must enter into that silent presence.

8.2 The Way of Stillness

To meditate, you must learn to be still. Meditation is perfect stillness of body and spirit.

Stillness is our way to rootedness, to be rooted in our true self, to be rooted in the gift that God has given us in our own being. So we must learn to be still in the one place. Becoming rooted in ourselves, we become rooted in our own proper place in creation and, as a result, rooted in our Creator. As St Paul puts it, the challenge of our life, the task of our life, the aim of our life, is to become 'rooted in Christ'. And he dwells in our hearts. This is why we have to become rooted in our own hearts. The outward silence and the outward stillness is just a sign of the inner stillness, the inner silence, the inner rootedness. And so, whether you are meditating on your own at home, or here with a group, be still. Be as still as you can be.

That means, when you sit down, choose a really alert posture, with your spine upright; place your arms and hands in some comfortable way. Then stay absolutely still. There will be the temptation to scratch your nose or straighten your collar or tie or glasses. You will have all sorts of longing – to stroke your beard if you have one, or whatever it may be. But ignore everything. You can even encounter some physical discomfort. If you are young enough and supple enough, some kind of cross-legged position with the spine upright and the whole body together in a very disciplined way would be an excellent posture to go for. When you are beginning this, you may encounter some physical pain, as well as the urge to scratch your nose. But you have to try to go through that as far as you can. If you are learning to sit in the lotus position, it would be wise to practise outside of meditation, and then to sit in an alert cross-legged position to begin with, and not undertake the lotus position during meditation until you have some sort of expertise in it.

All of us, at some time during our meditation, will feel like moving. Not moving, staying still, may be our first lesson in transcending desire, transcending that fixation that we so often have with ourselves. So I want you to understand that meditation does involve this discipline. The first discipline you probably have to learn is to sit still, to be still.

The posture and the stillness is of supreme importance. It is an outward sign of your inner commitment to the discipline of meditation. The stillness of body, we achieve by sitting still.

And then the stillness of spirit. The bodily stillness is not the most difficult. It is the stillness of spirit; it's going beyond thinking, considering, analysing.

The Indian mystic, Sri Ramakrishna, who lived in Bengal in the nineteenth century, used to describe the mind as a mighty tree filled with monkeys, all swinging from branch to branch in an incessant riot of chatter and movement. When you begin to meditate, you recognize that as a wonderfully apt description of the constant whirl going on in our mind. Prayer is not a matter of adding to this confusion by trying to shut it down and covering it with another lot of chatter. The task of meditation is to bring all of this mobile and distracted mind to stillness, silence and concentration, to bring it into its proper service. This is the aim given to us by the psalmist: "Be still and know that I am God." (Psalm 46:10)

To achieve this aim, we use a very simple device. It's one which St Benedict drew to the attention of his monks as far ago as the sixth century by directing them to read the Conferences of John Cassian. Cassian recommended anyone who wanted to learn to pray, and to pray continually, to take a single short verse and just to repeat this verse over and over again. In the Tenth Conference, he urges this method of simple and constant repetition of a short verse as the best way of casting out all distractions, all monkey chatter from our mind, in order that it might rest in God.

Alert stillness is not a state of consciousness familiar to most Westerners. We tend either to be alert or relaxed. Rarely are the two states combined in most of us. But in meditation, we come to experience ourselves as at one and the same time totally relaxed and totally alert. This stillness is not the stillness of sleep, but rather of totally awakened concentration.

If you look at a watchmaker about to perform some deft movement with a fine pair of tweezers, you will notice how still and poised he is as he scrutinizes the inside of the watch through his eyeglass. His stillness, however, is one of complete concentration, serious absorption in what he is doing. Similarly in meditation, our stillness is not a state of mere passivity but a state of full openness, full wakefulness to the wonder of our own being, full openness to the wonder of God, the author and sustainer of our being, and a full awareness that we are at one with God.

8.3 The Way of Simplicity

The way of meditation is a way of great simplicity. In the sort of society that we live in, we are not used to putting our total trust and faith in something that is very, very simple. We have all been brought up to trust really complex things. So when we approach something like meditation, we tend to get interested in the techniques that are involved. Well, the techniques have their place. But it is not the first thing to turn your mind to when you are learning to meditate. The most important thing when you are beginning is to understand the absolute simplicity of it. Then, to remain faithful to the simplicity of the practice.

The first thing you must learn when you set out on the pilgrimage of meditation is to listen to the message with the simplicity of a child. When we meditate, we go beyond desire, beyond possessiveness, beyond self-importance.

This is from the Gospel of St Luke:

They even brought babies for him to touch, but when the disciples saw them they scolded them for it. But Jesus called for the children and said, 'Let the little ones come to me. Do not try to stop them. For the Kingdom of God belongs to such as these. I tell you that whoever does not accept the Kingdom of God like a child will never enter it.' (Luke 18:15-17)

Meditation is the way of rediscovering our sense of wonder. Christian prayer is a state of innocence. You must transcend, and you must come to your meditation with childlike simplicity. "Unless you become like little children, you cannot enter the Kingdom of Heaven." (Matt 18:3)

Simplicity, being simple, is not necessarily easy for us. One of the difficulties for people who want to learn to meditate is just this. They ask, "What do you have to do to meditate?" When they are told that you have to sit still and you have to learn just to say one word or one short phrase, people are often scandalized. I have had people say to me, "Well, I've got a Ph.D. in advanced physics. That may be all right for the common people but surely for me there must be something a little more demanding than that." But that is the essence of meditation – to learn to be silent, to learn to be still.

You have to learn to say your word. It is difficult because this is not the conventional wisdom. Most people in our society think of wisdom as growing in complexity, and the more abstruse and rarefied the ideas that you can examine and master, the wiser you will become. If you say to someone, "I am going just to sit down every morning and every evening and I am going to learn to say this word", many people will say to you, "Well you must be a fool. Surely life is too precious, and time too precious for you to waste time, half an hour in the morning and half an hour in the evening, just saying a word like this. Weren't you given your mind for something more worthy, something better than that?" So it takes a good deal of courage for each of us, as men and women of the twentieth century, actually to sit down and to meditate, every morning and every evening. But that is what is required.

So my advice to you is: Say your word, be content to say your word, and allow the gift to be given by God. Don't demand it. We should come to our meditation with no demands and no expectations, but just that generosity of spirit that summons us to be as present as we can, to ourselves and to God.

The task we face is to become simple enough, humble enough simply to say our word, simply to return to saying our word and leaving behind all thought and imagination at the time of meditation. There are other times for reflection, for analysis, but those times are not the times of meditation. During the time of meditation, we must learn to be like little children, to be childlike, to be content with saying our word and letting go of all thought, of all imagination and of all analysis.

Saying our mantra, every morning and every evening, is just this entry into a childlike state where we place our full confidence and trust in God. Whatever gift he gives us, we receive with simplicity and joy. Whatever barrenness he leads us through, we accept with the same simplicity and joy. And the greatest joy there is, is to enter into this oneness, a oneness in which all desire leaves us, a oneness that brings us into complete harmony, a harmony with our own spirit, with the Spirit of God, and with all creation.

8.4 The Way of Discipline

You can't learn to meditate unless you build it into your life as a regular pattern, as a regular discipline. It requires considerable sacrifice to find that time every morning and evening, considerable discipline, but it is necessary. It is necessary because the presence of God, in his universe, in his creation, in your heart and my heart, is of such importance that we ignore it at our peril. If we ignore it, we can never make sense of either ourselves or the universe. That's why the journey requires seriousness and discipline, and that seriousness and discipline will lead you to a peace and to a joy that no words can possibly describe.

My recommendation to you is, in your daily meditation, to start with a minimum meditation of twenty minutes. Try as soon as you can to put it to twenty-five; the ideal time is about half an hour. And take the same time, whether it is twenty, twenty-five or thirty minutes – the same time-slot – every day. It's very useful, I think, to take a precise time slot and say, "OK, I am going to meditate for twenty minutes", and when the twenty minutes is over, to get up and end the meditation. The temptation is to prolong the meditation when it is going well, and when it is going badly to shorten it. The really important thing is to take a step away from that self-consciousness and impose an absolute limit. The discipline of meditation is of supreme importance.

If you want to learn to meditate, it is absolutely necessary to meditate every day. Every day of your life, every morning and every evening. There are no short cuts. There are no crash courses. There is no instant mysticism. It is simply the gentle and gradual change of direction, the change of heart.

To meditate, each of us must learn to be still, and that is a discipline. Meditation does involve this discipline – to sit still, to be still. The body then becomes an outward sign of the inward stillness that you approach in your pilgrimage as you say the mantra.

You must never forget the way to say your mantra from the beginning to the end. That is basic, axiomatic, and let no one dissuade you from the truth of that. In your reading, you may come across all sorts of variants and alternatives. But the discipline, the ascesis, of meditation places that one demand on us absolutely: that we must leave self behind so completely, leave our thoughts, analyses and feelings behind so completely, so as to be totally at the disposition of the Other. We must do that in an absolute way. That is the demand that the mantra makes upon us: to say it from beginning to the end, in all simplicity and in absolute fidelity.

People sometimes say to me, "What is the technique that you teach?" In the modern world, we are used to thinking about techniques. Life presents us with a series of problems, each of which needs a technique to solve it. But what I want to suggest to you, right at the beginning of your own pilgrimage, is that meditation is not a technique. Meditation is a discipline. It is the discipline of the disciple, open to the Master, alert, present and reverent as we come into his presence.

8.5 The Way of Commitment

The challenge that each of us has to face in our life is to become wholly committed to what is eternal. And so the essential challenge that each of us has to face and meet is to root and found our lives on eternal, enduring reality. And this is God.

In meditation we enter into the basic relationship of our life. God, our Creator and our Father, calls us into an intimacy with him that arises because he knows us and loves us. And, in this process of knowing and loving us, he invites us to come into a relationship of knowledge and love with him.

What we discover as we persevere in our meditation is that we cannot put God into a waiting room and say to him, "When I'm through with this important business I'm engaged in, I'll attend to you." We cannot put God on hold and say, "I'll be back in a minute." As we commit ourselves to meditate every morning and evening, we discover that we have to learn to pay attention to God *now*, today.

To learn to meditate, you have to understand that it is a daily commitment. A commitment that goes totally beyond what we feel. We do not meditate when we feel like it, or not meditate when we do not feel like it. We accept the discipline of the daily meditation, and the daily return to it. Then we accept the discipline of the word, of the mantra, the recitation of it from beginning to end.

This is a reading from the letter of St Paul to the Colossians:

> *Whatever you are doing put your whole heart into it, as if you were doing it for the Lord and not for men, knowing that there is a Master who will give you your heritage as a reward for your service.* (Col 3:23-4)

Put your whole heart into it. Meditation calls us to a deep level of understanding. Once we begin to meditate, once we have taken the first steps, we realize that we can no longer remain in the shallows. The call is for a complete reorientation of our being, a radical conversion. The call is, above all else, to enter the mystery itself, to learn what cannot be learned elsewhere. For this call to be answered, every part of our being has to be involved.

At a certain point I think we are all tempted to give up. We are unsettled by the absolute nature, both of the mystery of God itself, and by the absolute nature of the path of meditation. All of us are tempted to hold back. We like to hang on to our familiar illusions. All of us, too, like to keep our options open.

There are no half measures. You can't decide to do a *bit* of meditation. The option is to meditate and to root your life in reality. As far as I can understand it, that is what the Gospel is about. That is what Christian prayer is about: a commitment to life, a commitment to eternal life. As Jesus himself puts it, the Kingdom of Heaven is here and now. What we have to do is to be open to it, to be committed to it.

The way of limitless life requires on our part openness, generosity and simplicity. Above all, it requires commitment. Not commitment to a cause or to an ideology, but commitment to the simplicity in our own lives of the daily return to the roots of our own existence. A commitment to respond to life with attention, to create the space in our own lives to live fully.

What we learn in meditation, in the silence of it and in the simplicity of it, is that we have nothing to fear from the commitment to creating this space. I think all of us fear commitment because it seems to be a reducing of our options. We say to ourselves, "Well, if I commit myself to meditating, then I'll not be able to do other things." But what all of us find in the commitment to be serious, to be open, to live not out of the shallows of our being but out of its depths, what we all find in the experience of meditation is that our horizons are expanding, not contracting. We find not constraint but liberty.

8.6 The Way of Leaving Self Behind

These are the words of Jesus that are recorded in the Gospel of Luke:

If anyone wishes to be a follower of mine, he must leave self behind; day after day, he must take up his cross and follow me. Whoever cares for his own safety is lost; but if a man will let himself be lost for my sake, that man is safe. (Luke 9:23-24)

The big problem for us in trying to understand the Gospel is to understand its paradox. If we want to find our lives, we must be prepared to lose them.

Somehow or other, each of us, if we want to come to the truth, must find that delicate balance between self-abandonment and self-fulfilment. The balance is of extreme importance because if we go solely for self-fulfilment, we are likely to become a very insufferable person seeing everything, all reality, all relationships, only in terms of our own self-fulfilment. If, on the other hand, we go only for self-abandonment, we are likely to be perhaps equally insufferable too seeing our lives and ourselves as martyrs, as constantly denying our life.

Now what Jesus is talking about is a balance: self-abandonment and self-fulfilment. And we have to discover within ourselves that delicate point of balance. The curious thing about abandonment and fulfilment is that there is no fulfilment without abandonment. You all know from your own experience that the great problem with all of us is to allow ourselves to be loved. It is only when we allow ourselves to be loved that we can ourselves love. The big problem in every human life is taking this first step of allowing oneself to be loved.

This is abandonment. This is leaving self behind. This is transcending self. What follows is love. This is fulfilment. This is the absolute discovery of self, in the other, beyond oneself.

Jesus achieved his mission by total abandonment of self, by handing over his life to the Father: "Not my will but thy will be done." That is exactly the way for all of us. That is the precise purpose of all meditation. To lose our lives, to lose ourselves, and to become totally absorbed in God through the human consciousness of Jesus. Meditation is a powerful way if we can learn to say the mantra continually, ceaselessly, because that is the way in prayer to leave self behind, to lay down our life so as to be absorbed in the infinite mystery of God.

What meditation does is to take us into the life of God. This is why meditation is an entry into divinization through Jesus. Through him, we become one with God. Through him, we utterly transcend ourselves, leaving the whole of ourselves behind, and becoming a new creation in him. Meditation is itself the process of self-transcendence. To the degree that we are transcending ourselves we are divine, because we are learning to become one with the power of love. Each of us, by our own little self-transcendence, is nevertheless empowered to become one with God. This is what we must never forget.

8.7 The Way of Faith

This is a reading from St Paul's letter to the Hebrews:

And what is faith? Faith gives substance to our hopes, and makes us certain of realities we do not see. It is for their faith that the men of old stand on record. By faith we perceive that the universe was fashioned by the Word of God, so that the visible came forth from the invisible. (Heb. 11:1-3)

Meditation is of supreme importance for us because it takes us into the experience of faith. Faith is simply openness to and commitment to the spiritual reality which is beyond ourselves and yet in which we have our being. By faith we go beyond what is visible to the invisible, the spiritual reality.

Our faith is faith in what the synoptic Gospels (Matthew, Mark and Luke) call 'the Kingdom of God.' The Kingdom of God is simply God's power enthroned in our hearts. This is what Christian joy is about, that that power of God is rooted in our heart unshakably. Nothing, no powers, no dominations, nothing can loosen that rootedness of faith. The Kingdom we are given is unshakable. As Christians we have to be able to communicate that Kingdom and that faith. But we can only do so if the reality of that Kingdom is not just known to us, but embedded in the bedrock of our being.

Later on, in the letter to the Hebrews, the authors say:

We must run with resolution the race for which we are entered, our eyes fixed on Jesus, on whom faith depends from start to finish. (Heb. 12:1-2)

That is what faith is about. It is opening our eyes to that larger reality, the reality that is revealed in Jesus, who reveals to us the Father. Our eyes are taken off ourselves. When we meditate we are not concerned with ourselves, with our own perfection or our own wisdom or our own happiness. Our eyes are fixed on Jesus, and we receive from him everything, everything that we need to run the race and everything that we need to make light of the difficulties we have, whatever they are. Jesus who, "for the sake of the joy that lay ahead of him, endured the cross, making light of its disgrace, and has now taken his seat at the right hand of the throne of God." (Heb 12:2) Meditation does make us 'light of heart', because we know that there is only one thing essential to life and that is that we ourselves are fully open to and fully in harmony with the author of life, the Word through whom we have our being, the incarnate Son of God, our Lord Jesus.

What really matters is our faith, our deep commitment to Christ at the very bedrock of our being. That's what matters.

The clear message of the New Testament is that Jesus Christ is essential and that what he communicates to us is his own being. As Christians we must be utterly serious in our commitment to the gift that is given us: the gift of our life and the gift of our redemption, that we are made one with God in Jesus. As Christians we should be proclaiming this gospel to the whole world saying that each of us is made for this destiny of oneness, of fullness of life. That is the essence of the Christian proclamation. We must understand that this is now accomplished in Jesus, if only we will realize it.

Meditation is our acceptance of the gift, the gift of our life, the gift of Jesus and the gift of his Spirit. Because the gift is infinite, it requires our full attention, our full concentration. This is what Christianity is about – the full acceptance of that gift of liberty, that we are made free in Christ Jesus. Christianity is not so much obeying this law or that law, fulfilling this obligation or that obligation. It is coming to the whole of life with our hearts filled with wonder at what is, at what has been achieved, in Jesus.

But we must be serious. We must be committed. In St Paul's words, we must have faith. We can only have faith, and be committed, when we enter into the experience personally, when we let go of our own thoughts and plans and feelings and plunge into the depths of the mystery of God.

That is exactly what saying the mantra leads us to. That is why we must say it so faithfully. Now, when you begin, you have to take it on faith that the recitation of the word is a significant activity. You have to take it on faith that the journey of meditation is a journey into depth of understanding, depth of experience, an utter conviction in the reality in which we are rooted. We make our act of faith on the authority of a tradition that men and women have trodden this path throughout the ages and have done so with generosity, with love and fidelity and, in the process, have been brought to understanding, to compassion, to wisdom.

Now when you begin, you have to begin in faith, and you have to continue in faith. Every time you sit down to meditate, your faith will be tested and so your faith will be strengthened. The time of meditation, when you say your mantra from beginning to end, might often seem to you to be a complete waste of time, a complete loss of time, but remember Jesus dwells in your heart. he is the revelation of God. Only in God and only from God do we have our reality.

Beginning to meditate is like drilling for oil in the desert. The surface is so dry and so dusty that you have to take on faith the findings of the geologists who tell you that, deep within this dry earth, there is a great source of power. When we begin to meditate for the first time, we cannot help expecting something to happen -- that we will see some vision, come to some deeper knowledge -- but nothing happens. And it really is because 'nothing happens' that you can be sure that you are on the right path, the path of simplicity, of poverty, of surrender.

Jesus has told us that his Spirit is to be found in our hearts. Meditating is uncovering this truth, this reality deep within ourselves. The Spirit that we are invited to discover in our hearts is the power source that enriches every part of our lives.

8.8 The Way of Trust

Meditation is the great way of trust. We sit down, we sit still, we say our mantra with growing fidelity, and trust our whole selves utterly to God. We do that every morning and every evening of our lives. Thus we learn to live out of that trust.

You cannot be a Christian unless you learn to trust absolutely. What every one of us can find out from our own experience is that, at the moment of trust, the trickle of life becomes a torrent. The reason is that this act of trust starts the process of breaking down the barriers of our own ego, and our Christian life, the power of the life of Christ within us is something that is constantly expanding, constantly growing in our hearts.

I was reading the other day of the Indian god Shiva, who was sitting with his wife looking down on the world and his wife said to him, "Why don't you go and grant salvation to some of your devotees?" Shiva said, "Very well." So they went down to a town and they sat in the market place. The word got around that the great prophet was there. Then the holy men of the town came out. The first of them came up to Shiva and he said, "I meditate eight hours every day. In winter, I meditate for two hours in cold water. In summer, I meditate for two hours in the heat. When will I get salvation?" Shiva looked at him and he said, "Three more incarnations". You can just imagine the story as this man goes back to his friends shaking his head, "Three more! three more!" And so it goes on. Another man comes and he is told he will have ten more incarnations.

Finally, a little man comes and he says, "I am afraid I don't do much, but I try to love everyone around me, and I try to love creation. Can I get salvation?" Shiva scratches his head and the little fellow gets a little nervous and asks again, "Can I get salvation?" Shiva looks at him and says, "Well, a thousand incarnations," at which this little fellow jumps in delight and joy and starts shouting to everyone, "I will get it, I will get salvation! A thousand, only a thousand!" And at that, he bursts into flames and so do Shiva and his wife, and they all become one flame and are gone. Shiva's wife says to him, "How did that little old man get salvation immediately? You said a thousand incarnations." Shiva said, "Yes, that was my ruling. But his generosity overruled my ruling. So he was saved immediately."

Just after I read that, I picked up the Gospel of Luke and this was what I read in Luke:

> *Two men went up to the temple to pray, one a Pharisee and the other a tax gatherer. The Pharisee stood up and prayed thus: 'I thank thee, O God, that I am not like the rest of men, greedy, dishonest, adulterous or for that matter like this tax gatherer. I fast twice a week. I pay tithes on all that I get.' But the other kept his distance and would not even raise his eyes to heaven, but beat his breasts saying,' O God, have mercy on me, sinner that I am.' (Luke 18:10-14)*

I think meditation is a way that we follow to entrust ourselves utterly to the mystery of our own existence. To be meditating is simply to be in the state of accepting all as it is. As you know, by learning to say your mantra, in absolute simplicity, we entrust our whole being to him. Meditating is in many ways a sacrificial act. We lay ourselves on the line. We offer ourselves to God, abandoning everything that we are, and everything by which we know that we are. We simply say our mantra.

Meditation is an entrance into the nearness of God. He is to be found in our own hearts. God answers the yearning of our heart with the simple answer of love. His love is our hope, our unshakable confidence that whatever the difficulty, whatever the challenge, we can meet it out of the infinite resources he gives us. He does all this within us in silence, if only we will allow the mystery to encompass us. The quality that we require for this work is simply acceptance of everything that is: trust.

8.9 The Way of Love

Meditation is the way of love because its end is communion: a common union, Jesus and ourselves united to the Father. The man or woman of prayer is a man or woman in communion, in communion with love, in communion with God.

The greatest theological statement ever made was made by St John when he said: "God is love."

In meditation as Christians our hearts are directed towards God's love. What each of us has to remember, and to know with absolute clarity and certainty is that we are infinitely loveable and infinitely loved. We must know that not just as an intellectual proposition but we must know it with experiential knowledge, in our own hearts. It is the most important knowledge there is for any of us. That is why meditation is so important, so that we can fasten our minds and hearts upon *the* essential fact of history, the knowledge that God is love.

This is what Jesus came to proclaim, and he came to do more than proclaim it. He came to establish this knowledge in your heart and in mine. To be a Christian is to live out of that conviction. But we cannot live out of it unless we know it. That is why we return to the humble task of saying our mantra every morning and every evening.

Love involves a total acceptance of the other, an acceptance that is entirely unconditional. It is an acceptance of the other that is so total that the self is lost.

There is only the other. The wonder of it is that we find ourself loved. There is a real sense in which we can say that, unless we are loved, we can never find ourself. Now consider this in relation to meditation. The saying of the mantra is an act of pure selflessness. Every time we say the mantra, we renounce, we leave behind our own thoughts, our own concerns, our own hopes, our own fears. In saying the mantra, we become "the eye that sees but that cannot see itself".

In saying our mantra, in the daily return to the discipline, we gradually learn to look beyond ourselves. We learn to see with a vision that focuses itself ahead of us, in God. In that focusing of everything in God, everything that we are, everything in our life, becomes aligned on God and everything falls into its own proper place.

Meditating is powerful because it does lead us into this order, into this tranquillity, into this peace. This is so because our order of values is changed. Instead of our values system being based on the self, on the ego, on success, on self-promotion, on these limiting factors, our values system becomes based on God. We discover, in the revelation that takes place in our heart, the revelation when we discover the presence of Jesus there, that God is love. This brings us to the conclusion that unleashes great power – that there is only one thing that matters ultimately, which is that we grow in love. Everything else is secondary. Everything else is consequential. Once this insight becomes powerful enough, our lives become altered. We see the importance of compassion, of understanding. We begin, therefore, to become really sensitive people who are in touch with life at its centre. And remember, God is the centre, God is love, and Jesus is the revelation of this love.

This is not just some beautiful theory. It is the most practical consequence of a very practical practice, the practice of meditating every day of our lives, every morning and every evening. For that half an hour, every morning and every evening, we are focused beyond ourselves. Our spirit is expanding, our heart is enlarging, we are becoming more generous.

The change in us comes about because, in meditation, we encounter the power to make this change possible. All of us would like to be more kind, more understanding, more selfless, more sympathetic, more compassionate, and so on. But, at the same time, we recognize ourselves as weak, mortal, fallible human beings. What we discover in meditation is the power source to enable us to live this way. We discover that this power source is established right at the centre of our own being, in our own hearts. "God is the centre of my soul."

The great mystery of the Christian faith is that this love is to be found in your own heart, if only you can be silent and still, and if only you can make this love the supreme centre of your being. That means turning to it wholeheartedly, paying attention to it. You approach your life with love because what you encounter in your own heart is the living principle of love. Listen to St Paul suggesting how we should be in our relationships with one another:

> *Be forbearing with one another, and be forgiving, where any of you has cause for complaint: you must forgive as the Lord forgave you.* [Then he goes on.] *To crown all, there must be love, to bind all together and complete the whole.* (Col 3:13-15)

The most important thing that we as Christians have to proclaim to the world, to proclaim to everybody, is that this Spirit does indeed dwell in our hearts. By turning to it with full attention, we too can live out of this fullness of love. We too can live out of this power that is the Kingdom of God. Part of the discipline of saying the mantra is that it teaches us to stay in that love, come what may. Nothing will shake us from our conviction that God is, that God is Love and that his love dwells in our hearts.

8.10 The Way of Wisdom

Wisdom is simply the gift of distinguishing between illusion and reality.

Just listen to St Paul:

I pray that the God of our Lord Jesus Christ, the all-glorious Father, may give you the spiritual powers of wisdom and vision, by which there comes the knowledge of him. I pray that your inward eyes may be illumined, so that you may know what is the hope to which he calls you. (Eph 1:17-18)

The knowledge we come to in meditation is not just simply new additions to the memory bank. The knowledge we come to is wisdom – to know the significance of what we know, to know in perspective. Wisdom is simply knowing with a divine perspective; knowing everything in the perspective of eternity.

Wisdom is the capacity to focus on the real and to reject illusion, or at least to identify illusion as illusion, as trivial, as passing, as shallow, as two-dimensional. The truly spiritual man or woman is the person who has focal depth, who can see things in their relationships because everything is seen in its relation to the divine centre. We need this wisdom and we need it absolutely if we are to live our lives fully, sincerely, earnestly and lovingly. To live our life lovingly we must be in contact with love as the source of our being.

To enter this wisdom, we must learn how to become recollected. We must collect ourselves together. We must become mindful, remember who we are and where we are and why we are. We need to find a peace within ourselves. This peace, this mindfulness, this recollection will enable us to commence this focusing on the divine centre, the centre from which everything flows and unto which everything flows. Meditation is getting into harmony with that great flow of life from him, with him, to him.

By focusing our whole being, our whole attention, on the divine centre that is to be found at the same time in our own hearts and utterly beyond us in the depth of God, this very act of focusing leads us to wisdom and so to the knowledge of what in life is important, to distinguish what is serious and what is essential from what is trivial or frivolous, or passing.

One of the things that we must understand is that this meditation, this pursuit of wisdom and love, must take place in an entirely ordinary, natural way. Meditation must be built into the ordinary fabric of everyday life. We must learn to see the whole of life shot through with the divine, in harmony with the divine. The spiritual quest, the spiritual invitation is getting our lives, ourselves, into focus with ultimate truth, not in any self-important way, but in a very simple childlike way. It is by being still, by paying attention and by becoming mindful of the one who loves us.

To be fit for the great tasks in life, we must learn to be faithful in humble tasks. Meditation is a very simple and very humble pilgrimage that prepares us for this focusing of our lives on the divine centre. Our lives are nourished by the sap, the energy rising from the root of all being. Every morning of our lives and every evening of our lives, we settle down. We recollect ourselves. We become mindful. We turn ourselves in the direction of the divine centre. We focus ourselves. We do so by the simple expedient of saying our word. We banish all the images that create a wall between ourselves and reality, by smashing all the symbols and allowing the pure, brilliant light of reality, the clear brilliant light of God's Spirit 'shining', as St Paul puts it, in our hearts, to allow that to become the supreme reality for us.

This task is not too hard for us. We don't have to travel over the sea to find it. We do not have to ask others to do it for us. This reality is very near us. It is in our hearts if only we will take the trouble to seek first the Kingdom of God, the Kingdom that is in our hearts, the Kingdom that Jesus himself has established in our hearts. That requires simple fidelity, faithfulness, common sense, the common sense that tells us we must return constantly to drink, and to drink deeply at this fountain of life. Drinking deeply there, everything in our lives comes into focus, once we are focused on that divine centre.

Listen to St Paul:

Therefore, my brothers, I implore you by God's mercy, to offer your very selves to him: a living sacrifice, dedicated and fit for his acceptance, the worship offered by mind and heart. Adapt yourselves no longer to the pattern of this present world, but let your minds be remade and your whole nature thus transformed. Then you will be able to discern the will of God, and to know what is good, acceptable and perfect. (Rom 12:1-2)

This is a wonderful description of meditation: "Let your minds be remade." Saying the mantra is, as it were, wiping clean the slate of consciousness so that our consciousness may be filled with the knowledge of the love of God. It is this fullness that transforms us, transforms our whole nature. Being transformed, the will of God is clear, and we seek what is good and perfect.

8.11 The Way of Enlightenment

One of the words that is used to describe the purpose of meditation is the word 'enlightenment'. We become 'enlightened'. St John in his Gospel describes the purpose of the coming of Christ as being to banish the darkness. He speaks of the power of Christ's light being so great that the darkness cannot overcome it, cannot quench it.

All of us are aware that there is much darkness in our world. We hear every day of terrible injustices, of violence, of hatred, of feuds, of greed and so on. We see this both at the personal level and indeed at the international level. All of us too are aware of the darkness within ourselves. We recognize that we too have a dark side. We too have a capacity to live at a level that we know is not really worthy of our human destiny as persons.

When we begin to meditate, we begin to understand that we cannot enter into the experience of meditation with just a part of our being. Everything that we are, the totality of our being, must be involved in this entry into wholeness, our own personal wholeness and harmony. Another way of saying this is that every part of our being must be open to the light. Every part of us must come into the light. We do not meditate just to develop our religious side or our religious capacity. The truly spiritual man or woman is in harmony with every capacity they have. That is why the truly spiritual man or woman does everything that they do with the greatest possible perfection, the greatest possible love, and so the greatest possible joy.

Meditation is not the process whereby we try to see the light. In this life we cannot see the light fully and continue to live. Meditation is the process whereby we come into the light, the process whereby we begin to see everything, the whole of reality. We begin to see it all by the power of the light. What Jesus tells us is that the power of the 'light' is love. The test of our progress in meditation is how far we are moving into this condition of seeing everyone and everything by the light of God. Seeing by the light of love makes us loving toward them all, too. Not judging, not rejecting, but seeing everyone and the whole of creation by this light which we must discover in our own hearts.

Make time available every morning and every evening of our life. For that time we must be open to the light, to God, to love. Not thinking our own thoughts, not planning our own plans, but entering into an ever more profound silence, an ever more profound reverence, our being becoming rooted in God.

Recite your word, your mantra peacefully and calmly and allow the word to sink deep into your being. It builds up a resonance within you, every part of your own being in resonance with God. As we enter into that resonance, we ourselves enter into the light of his love.

The message given to us by Jesus is that every one of us in this room is called ultimately not only to see by the light, but our ultimate call is to see the light itself. At that moment we become totally at one with the light. That's the moment when, as St Peter puts it, "we share in the very being of God".

Listen to St Paul writing to the Corinthians:

The same God who said, 'Out of darkness let light shine', has caused his light to shine within us, to give the light of revelation – the revelation of the glory of God, in the face of Jesus Christ. (2 Cor 4:6)

The way of meditation is the way of opening ourselves as fully as we can in this life to Jesus Christ. He is our light. He is our enlightenment. The fullness of his Spirit dwells in our hearts, and the task of Christians is to understand this in all its power and wonder in the depth of our spirit. Our gospel, the gospel that we preach, is a gospel of the glory of Christ, a glory that shines throughout history, and a glory that shines in each of us. The light of that glory is the light that gives direction to the lives of each one of us.

When we meditate every morning and evening, we set everything else aside and we are open to that light. We seek to follow that light and to be illumined by it. The marvel of meditation is that, if we can be faithful to that meditation, everything in our lives that is not consonant with the light is burned away by it.

8.12 The Way of Peace

I want to talk to you about meditation as the way of peace, the way to peace. Just listen to these words of St Paul:

Your world was a world without hope and without God. But now in union with Christ Jesus, you who once were far off have been brought near through the shedding of Christ's blood. For he himself is our peace. (Eph 2:12-13)

In the New Testament, this peace is the greatest quality that we can possess. It's beyond understanding. But, for us to be able to enter into this peace, we must enter into the experience of meditation itself.

Peace is not a static quality. Peace is full vitality. It's the sense of joyous well-being that comes to us when we find ourselves to be truly harmonious, every part of our being in harmony. What you can discover by persevering in meditation is that not only our life has found its inner coherence (that is of course a necessary first step for each one of us) but it's something even greater than that. In meditation, we find our own inner resonance in God.

As monks, what we have to say to you is that no one must be content to live their life just at ten per cent of their potential. Each of us must live at a hundred per cent of our potential. We must enter into that profound inner resonance in God. It's not just that we are called to be resonant *with* God, but *in* him. This is our call, this is our destiny – to find peace beyond ourselves in God.

The great temptation for us today is to think of peace as a state that can be induced. Our culture tells us that we can induce any emotional state we like, by chemical means or by an act of the will. But peace understood in its spiritual significance, in its spiritual sense, is not something that can be induced, but it's something we must enter into. It's not something that anyone of us can command by exercising one or more of our faculties. But it's something that depends on a total correspondence between all our faculties, all our potentialities.

The peace that we want to see in the world is not something that can be imposed by force. You can force a person to put down his gun if you have more or bigger guns, but you can't force anyone to be peaceful. We ourselves can know no peace if we do not ourselves exercise this same gentleness, this same peacefulness ourselves. If you force your adversary at the point of a gun to be peaceful, you will always live in fear that he may become stronger than you, may develop some new secret weapon.

The only thing that can create peace in our world is the power of peace found, known, and experienced, in human hearts. This peace, once we know it ourselves as the very basis and foundation of our being, is invincible. It is stronger than any violence and stronger than any fear, because peace is creative. It is patient, it knows how to suffer whereas violence is impatient and destructive.

Now these truths we must all know from our own personal experience. We cannot find peace within ourselves by using any sort of violence against ourselves. We don't run off our fears, our self-rejection, our anxieties, our repressions, our insecurities, by any sort of violence.

We come to fullness of life by drinking deep at the fountain of life. That fountain of life is to be found springing up in our own hearts.

In the Christian vision, peace is not just a state of being. It is a person, Jesus Christ. He himself is our peace. In the Christian vision of the New Testament, peace arises from harmony, communion with God. "Peace is my gift to you," said Jesus. In his great address at the last supper reported by John, Jesus speaks of his return to the Father, and then he adds, "I have told you all this so that in me, you may find peace. (John 14:27, 16:33)

Meditation is our way to peace. A commitment to silence is the first step into finding this peace of Christ.

8.13 The Way of Attention

These are words from the Sermon on the Mount:

Set your mind on God's Kingdom and his justice before everything else and all the rest will come to you as well. (Matt 6:33)

To set our minds on God's Kingdom. In recent times, there have been two exceptional thinkers who have had a very important influence on our society. One of them is Simone Weil and the other E F Schumacher. Simone Weil thought that *the* most important quality we could acquire in our lifetime was what she described as 'selfless attention'. Fritz Schumacher came to the same conclusion. He described the selfless attention that Simone Weil speaks of simply as 'attention' – learning to attend. Both of them were influenced by the tradition from which we speak, the tradition of contemplative prayer, the tradition of meditation coming from the early monastic fathers.

This is the crucial lesson that we have to learn from meditation: to attend wholly and totally, to pay attention. We all know from reading the Sermon on the Mount that each of us must not only change but we must be transformed. We also know from reading St Paul that we can only be transformed in Christ, through Christ, and with Christ.

If you want to change something in your life, you have two broad possibilities open to you. You can try to will that change; you can try to redirect your life by acts of the will. I think most of us discover from our own experience that our wills are appallingly weak and shockingly inconstant. There is another way, and the other way is the way of total openness of the whole person. It is not the way of *intention*, but the way of *attention*.

You will remember perhaps when you first came to meditate how I told you of my weekend walks in the jungle when I was living in the Far East and how my Malay boys were always terrified that I would be eaten by a tiger. In mortal terror, with tremendous devotion, they used to come with me on these walks, and suddenly one of them would say, "There is a tiger." And we would all stand absolutely still and listen totally to what was in the air. We would listen not even for the tiger but just listen to everything. We knew that if we were distracted by listening to one thing in particular, some monkey chattering in the treetop, it could be the last distraction we would ever have.

Now the kind of total attentive listening that we experienced on those jungle walks is just the sort of attention that we need if we are to understand the words of Christ. I do not think it is too far-fetched, I do not think it is any exaggeration, to say that if we want to understand the Sermon on the Mount then we have to learn to attend.

We have to learn to pay attention. Why should this be so powerful? Why should this selfless attention that Simone Weil speaks of be so powerful? It is because in the act of attention we transcend the ego. Fully absorbed in our attention, we leave self behind. When you come to think of it, what is it that could possibly mislead us in any sort of apprehension of reality, what could mislead us, but the ego?

Learning to attend, we learn to see with absolute clarity what is before us. We learn to hear what is said to us. In other words, we learn to be fully open to reality. That is what Jesus asks of each of us. That is what he invites each of us to: a full empathy with divine love. Without such attention, without such selfless attention we can never pass over, never fully hear or see or experience what is.

Everything we see or hear or experience is distorted by the prism of our ego.

Learning to say the mantra, we learn to leave all our own limited, distorted perceptions behind. We become absorbed into the divine reality. This is the oneness that Jesus speaks of in his great priestly prayer in the Gospel of John: "that we may be one". The English medieval mystics spoke of prayer as the process of 'oneing', becoming one.

Now, saying the mantra is simply our beginning on the path to this selfless attention, the searchlight of consciousness off ourselves, forward. We become like the eye that cannot see itself, that sees all. We begin to see (and here is the extraordinary thing about the Christian vocation) we begin to see everything as Christ sees it. In other words, we begin to see it with his light.

Works by and about John Main

Books

Awakening, John Main, London, Medio Media/Arthur James, 1997

Christian Meditation: The Gethsemani Talks, John Main, The World Community for Christian Meditation, 1977; Medio Media, 1999; Singapore, Medio Media, 2007

Community of Love, John Main, London, Darton, Longman & Todd, 1990; New York, Continuum, 1999

Silence and Stillness in Every Season: Daily Readings with John Main, ed Paul Harris, London, Darton, Longman & Todd, 1997

Door to Silence: An Anthology for Christian Meditation, John Main, ed Laurence Freeman, Norwich, Canterbury Press, 2006

John Main: A Biography in Text and Photos, Paul Harris, Medio Media, 2001

John Main – By Those Who Knew Him, ed Paul Harris, London, Darton, Longman & Todd, 1991; Canada, Novalis, 1991; Singapore, Medio Media, 2007

John Main: Essential Writings, ed Laurence Freeman, New York, Orbis Books, 2002

Joy of Being: Daily Readings with John Main, ed Clare Hallward, London, Darton, Longman & Todd, 1987; USA, Templegate, 1988

Letters from the Heart, John Main, New York, Crossroad, 1982

Moment of Christ, John Main, London, Darton, Longman & Todd, 1984; New York, Crossroad, 1984

Monastery without Walls: The Spiritual Letters of John Main, ed Laurence Freeman, Norwich, Canterbury Press, 2006

The Heart of Creation, John Main, London, Darton, Longman & Todd, 1988; New York, Crossroad, 1988; New York, Continuum, 1998

The Inner Christ, John Main, London, Darton, Longman & Todd, 1987. (Combines *Word into Silence*, *Moment of Christ*, and *The Present Christ*)

The Present Christ, John Main, London, Darton, Longman & Todd, 1985; New York, Crossroad, 1985

The Way of Unknowing, John Main, London, Darton, Longman & Todd, 1989; New York, Crossroad, 1989

Word into Silence: A Manual for Christian Meditation, John Main, ed Laurence Freeman, London, Darton, Longman & Todd, 1980; New York, Paulist Press, 1981; New York, Continuum, 2001; Norwich, Canterbury Press, 2006

Word made Flesh, John Main, London, Darton, Longman & Todd, 1993; New York, Continuum, 1998

CDs / Cassette Tapes

Being on the Way, John Main, Medio Media, 1991

Christian Meditation: The Essential Teaching, John Main, Medio Media, 1991

Communitas, Volumes 1–5, John Main, Medio Media, 1991

Fully Alive, John Main, Medio Media, 1991

In the Beginning, John Main, Medio Media, l991

The Hunger for Depth and Meaning: Learning to Meditate with John Main, compiled Peter Ng, Singapore, Medio Media, 2007

The Life and Teachings of John Main, Laurence Freeman, Medio Media, 2002

The Christian Mysteries, John Main, Medio Media, 1991

The Door to Silence, John Main, Medio Media, 1991

The Last Conferences, John Main, Medio Media, 1991

Word made Flesh, John Main, Medio Media, 1991

About The World Community for Christian Meditation

www.wccm.org

The World Community for Christian Meditation (WCCM) took form in 1991. It continues John Main's legacy in teaching Christian meditation and his work of restoring the contemplation dimension of Christian faith in the life of the Church.

The Community is now directed by Laurence Freeman OSB, a student of John Main and a Benedictine monk of the Olivetan Congregation. The World Community has its International Centre and a retreat centre in London. There are a number of Centres in other parts of the world. The Community is thus a 'monastery without walls', a family of national communities and emerging communities in over a hundred countries. The foundation of this Community is the local meditation group, which meets weekly in homes, parishes, offices, hospitals, prisons, and colleges. The World Community works closely with many Christian churches.

Annually it runs the John Main Seminar and The Way of Peace. It also sponsors retreats, schools for the training of teachers of meditation, seminars, lectures, and other programmes. It contributes to interfaith dialogues particularly, in recent years, with Buddhists and Muslims. A quarterly spiritual letter with news of the Community is mailed and also available online. Weekly readings can be sent direct by email. Information on current programmes, connections to national coordinators and the location of meditation groups can be found on the Community website which also offers a range of online audio talks. This site is the hub of a growing family of internet presence: the websites of national communities and special interests, such as the teaching of meditation to children and the contemporary spirituality of priests.

Medio Media is the communication and publishing arm of The World Community for Christian Meditation and offers a wide range of books, audio, and videos to support the practice of meditation.

The World Community for Christian Meditation: www.wccm.org
Medio Media and online bookstore: www.mediomedia.org

The World Community For Christian Meditation
Centres/Contacts Worldwide

International Centre
The World Community for Christian Meditation
St Mark's
Myddelton Square
London, EC 1R 1XX
UK
Tel: +44 20 7278 2070
Fax: +44 20 7713 6346
Email: mail@wccm.org
www.wccm.org

FOR COUNTRIES NOT LISTED CONTACT INTERNATIONAL CENTRE

Australia
Australian Christian Meditation Community
PO Box 246
Uralla New South Wales 2358
Tel:+61 2 6778 3284
Email: leon@christianmeditationaustralia.org
www.christianmeditationaustralia.org

Belgium
Christelijk Meditatie Centrum
Beiaardlaan 1
B-1850 Grimbergen
Tel/Fax: +32 2 305 7513
Email: ccm@pandora.be
www.christmed.be

Brazil
Comunidade de Meditacao Crista
Caixa postal 62559
CEP 22252 Rio de Janeiro
Brasil
Tel: +55 21 2523 5125
Email: ana.fonseca@umusic.com
www.wccm.com.br

Canada
Christian Meditation Community
Canadian National Resource Centre
P.O. Box 552, Station NDG
Montreal, Quebec
H4A 3P9
Tel: +1 514 485 7928
Fax: +1 514 489 9899
Email: christianmeditation@bellnet.ca
www.meditatio.ca

Méditation Chretiénne du Québec
7400 boul. St. Laurent, Suite 526
Montréal, Québec H2R 2Y1
Tel: +1 514 525 4649
Fax: +1 514 525 8110
Email: medchre@bellnet.ca
www.meditationchretienne.ca

Chile
www.meditacioncristiana.cl

Czech Republic
www.krestanskameditace.com

France
Communauté Mondiale de
Méditants Chrétiens
126 rue Pelleport
75020 Paris
Tel: +33 1 40 31 89 73
Email: cmmc@wanadoo.fr
www.meditationchretienne.org

Germany
WCCM
Untere Leiten 12 d
82065 Baierbrunn
Tel: +49 89 68020914
Fax: +49 89 74424917
Email: hm.plotzki@gmx.de
www.wccm.de

India
Christian Meditation Centre
Kripa Foundation
Mt Carmel Church
81/A Chapel Road
Bandra (W)
Mumbai 400050
Tel: +91 22 640 5411
Fax: +91 22 643 9296
Email: frjoe@bom5.vsnl.net.in

Ireland
Christian Meditation Centre
4 Eblana Avenue
Dun Laoghaire
Co. Dublin
Tel: +353 1 280 1505
Fax: +353 1 280 8720
E-mail: fergalgmcloughlin@gmail.com
www.wccmireland.org

Italy
Comunità Mondiale per la
Meditazione Cristiana
Via Marche, 2/a
25125 Brescia
Tel: +39 030 224549
E-mail: wccmitalia@virgilio.it
www.meditazionecristiana.org

Japan
www.esuk.net/wccm

Latvia
www.jesus.lv

Malta
www.wccmalta.org

Mexico
La Communidad Mundial de
Meditacion Cristiana
Paseo de Golondrinas Closter 11-401
C.P. 40880
Ixtapa, Guerrero
Ubifone: 800-1320 1320
Tel: +52 755 55 3 01 20
E-mail: lucia_gayon@yahoo.com
www.meditacioncristiana.com

Netherlands
www.wccm.nl